James Gleeson was born in Ireland, but has lived in London for 40 years. He has been a journalist and writer for all that time, working on a variety of newspapers and periodicals national, local and sporting. He has also been a director of a news agency. His published works include a number of radio scripts, including one of Britain's underwater war of 1939–45, which, with Tom Waldron, he subsequently expanded into a book entitled *The Frogman. Now it can Be Told* was also written in collaboration with Tom Waldron, and *Bloody Sunday* told the story of the Anglo-Irish war of 1916–22. Gleeson served in the army during the war, and later met many of the women secret agents through compiling a series of broadcasts on their war experiences. Married, with five children, he now lives in Hertfordshire in a cottage called 'Wits End'

They Feared No Evil

THE WOMAN AGENTS OF BRITAIN'S SECRET ARMIES 1939–45

James Gleeson

CORGI BOOKS
A DIVISION OF TRANSWORLD PUBLISHERS LTD

THEY FEARED NO EVIL

A CORGI BOOK 0 552 10655 0

Originally published in Great Britain by
Robert Hale & Co.

PRINTING HISTORY
Robert Hale edition published 1976
Corgi edition published 1978

This book is set in Plantin 10/11 pt.

Corgi Books are published by Transworld Publishers, Ltd.,
Century House, 61–63 Uxbridge Road, Ealing,
London, W5 5SA

Made and Printed in Great Britain by
Richard Clay (The Chaucer Press), Ltd., Bungay, Suffolk.

CONTENTS

ILLUSTRATIONS

FOREWORD

The British secret war department, called Special Operations Executive, was concerned with helping to organize and supply underground resistance forces in all enemy-occupied countries from 1941 to the end of hostilities in 1945.

The French section of SOE infiltrated thirty-nine women into France – by parachutes, aeroplanes and boats – between May 1941 and July 1944.

Fifteen of these women were captured by the Germans. Three survived imprisonment in concentration camps in Germany where the other tweleve were killed. One girl sickened and died in France.

The Free French parachuted eleven girls into France between January and September 1945. They all survived the war.

A hundred thousand native Frenchwomen were active with the Resistance during the war. Twelve thousand of them were captured and sent to prisons and concentration camps – only two thousand of those survived.

This book is concerned with the thirty-nine girls sent 'into the field' by Special Operations Executive and with another two thousand girls who worked secretly for SOE in Britain supporting those in the field.

In Parliament at Westminster on 6th March 1945 it was revealed for the first time that women had been recruited, trained and sent to France on active service.

In 1950 I met several of the girls who had returned and the relatives of many who had died. Their stories were told in a series of programmes which I wrote for the BBC.

This book is dedicated to all the women and girls who worked, suffered and died with and for the French Resistance 1939–1945.

James Gleeson

Yea, though I walk through the valley of the shadow of death
I shall fear no evil

23rd Psalm

1

Yvonne

Yvonne Baseden was twenty-two when she hurtled from an aircraft six hundred feet above the soil of France one fine but moonless night. It was very nearly midnight. The stars were bright in a cloudless sky but the countryside beneath was dark and featureless. The ex-secretary turned secret agent was on her way to her first assignment.

A few seconds behind her another figure emerged from the aircraft and began his descent to France. He was her commanding officer, Gonzagnes de St Genies. The dark countryside had been illuminated by brief signal lights a few minutes previously and the pilot recognizing them as the agreed and correct signals had instructed his two passengers to jump. Behind them other parachutes bearing supplies, a wireless transmitting set, weapons of war and mail came tumbling out. Now as Yvonne floated to earth she peered anxiously for pin-points of guiding lights from the flash-lamps of members of the French Resistance awaiting them on the ground. Even as she glimpsed them she was having a few anxious thoughts about her landing. This was her sixth parachute drop, but the five previous ones had been over friendly British countryside and some of them had finished in quite ridiculous fashions.

Because she was slim and so light parachutes sometimes wafted her away from the target areas. Once she had been deposited on the roof of the canteen at Ringway aerodrome and her companions had to obtain a ladder to rescue her. On another occasion she was one of a group who jumped at night. Her companions landed safely, but could not see her—they thought she had landed before them and gone back to her quarters, but when they arrived she was not there. They searched for two hours before they found her—dangling quite safely and calmly high up in the branches of a tall tree. This time she was all right—she landed perfectly, slipped off the parachute harness and began to fold the spreading silk.

She was now 'in the field', she was now not only in the war, she was at war, she was now wanted, hunted prey. Capture for her now meant not even the slight 'courtesies of war' extended to a captured soldier. It meant, she well knew, frightful treatment, torture if she would not betray her friends, and almost inevitably death. She was now a British agent in a countryside controlled and terrorized by efficient, alert and ruthless German forces. Yvonne had been well briefed on the risks and was keenly aware of them as she folded her parachute in the dark wood. Her reaction was automatic when she heard somebody crashing through the undergrowth towards her. She backed against a tree, drew her pistol and cocked it—whoever it was was making no attempt to approach quietly. Then came the noise of a stumble and fall—immediately the air was filled with a voluble flow of traditional French swear-words and she relaxed—only a genuine Frenchman, she knew, could swear like that. So she called out and was joined and embraced by the French farmer on whose ground she had landed.

He led her to the rest of the group, her officer was already there, and when they had collected the containers which the aircraft dropped, they trooped off to the farmer's house.

Amongst his many qualities Winston Churchill possessed a magnificent turn of phrase—some of them have already become clichés of the English language. One of them succinctly and unmistakeably in July 1940 explained and ordered Special Operations Executive's role in the existing conflict. 'Set Europe ablaze,' he said.

And well and truly did the newly formed department respond. It was founded in the dark days after Hitler had driven the British forces from the continent of Europe and when Hitler, as well as most of the rest of the world, was convinced that it was only a matter of weeks before the stubborn British capitulated. In fact even as the remnants of the British Expeditionary Forces were being rescued and landed on the southern shores of England, plans were being started for a return to the continent of Europe and for a confrontation there with the German army.

There was no precedent for such a department as Special Operation Executive because the need for one had never existed before. Hurriedly, a few professional soldiers with experience of guerrilla war and a few enthusiastic amateurs were called together and told to prepare Europe for the return bout. Their task was to aid and help organize the resistance forces which were bound to arise in the countries which the German armies occupied—the sooner the harassment of German forces began the better and once started it should increase in volume and intensity until the whole of occupied Europe was 'ablaze'.

The 'organization' as it was called by some, had a stormy birth. It was not welcomed by the traditional Secret Service departments, it was looked upon as an interloper and an inexperienced and rather shabby one at that. As we shall see however, the foundation members were men of no little talent, foresight and zeal. They were determined to carry out their orders no matter what the opposition and no matter whence it came. They had qualities of perseverance as well as being shrewd and had a totally unsuspected attitude of reserve towards traditional methods of warfare and its protagonists. They had no text books to study. They had to wage an unusual war in an unusual way and with unusual operatives. Having decided on their organizing and aggressive policies they set about recruiting the manpower, and later the womanpower, to carry their policies into effect.

'The Firm', as SOE was also called, had departments for each separate theatre of war. There were German, Belgian and Dutch departments amongst others. The one that we are dealing with was called the French section of SOE and so obviously it was of the highest importance that its operators should be fluent French speakers, best of all that they should be bilingual with English as the other language. Oddly enough it did not always work like this and some operators went 'into the field' with but the slightest, if any, knowledge of the French language.

It was essential that everything connected with the Firm should be top secret and this in itself made recruiting difficult. Having found a likely recruit he, or she, had to be told what it was about, the training and the frightful risks involved. If, after this, the recruit agreed to join 'on trial' he, or she, was subject to hard and rigorous tests phyically and psychologically. Not everyone who was accepted 'on trial' proved capable enough for acceptance, but by then, of course, the trainee knew a great deal about the organization, and could not just be sent back to their units or turned loose in civvy street. They were in fact retained incommunicado, in a remote hamlet, doing useful jobs in the war effort until sufficient time had passed for their knowledge to be so stale as to be useless. Then they were sent away. In recent years there has been one TV series called *The Village* which was founded on the plight of such people.

It was important therefore that even before a person was approached his, or her, background should be thoroughly explored. Several of the operatives were found in the armed services—including Yvonne Baseden. One summer's day in 1943 she opened a dull official envelope from the Ministry of Pensions asking her to present herself to an official at the Ministry in Whitehall, London. She told her friends who made a joke of it—'Not yet nineteen and they are going to pension you off,' said one. 'You are a lucky girl.'

Not yet nineteen, slim quiet Yvonne already knew a great deal about what German occupation meant. She was then a commissioned officer in the Women's Auxiliary Air Force working in the department which dealt with the allied Governments on all matters affecting their Air Forces, and supply of aircraft, training of personnel and co-ordination of plans. She was being constantly brought into touch with men who had escaped from enemy occupied territory and they all told similar stories of brutalities and oppression. She had seen the other side of the picture as well because after she had been commissioned in 1941 she had served with the RAF Intelligence branch and had assisted in the interrogation of captured airmen and submarine crews. Her shorthand and her knowledge of languages were useful. The Germans were winning well at that stage and were so confident—they even strutted in the prisoner-of-war cages!

She also met Frenchmen who had escaped to Britain to join the forces bringing very useful information about conditions with them. She knew all about the daily fear in which the French population lived, of being arrested, of disappearing, of being deported for work in Germany. She heard of the snap raids and the midnight hammering on the door, of how Jews had to wear a star to denote their 'racial impurity'. Yvonne's mother was French and Yvonne's connection with the country had begun long before her birth—during the days of the First World War.

Her father was an engineer who had joined the Royal Flying Corps—the predecessor of the Royal Air Force. He was flying an Avro fighter when he made a forced landing in France near a splendid château. He escaped unhurt from the aircraft and made his way to the château where he hoped there would be a telephone to enable him to contact his squadron. A butler answered the door and led him into the presence of the owner, the Countess de Vibrage. She was most kind and explained that there was, indeed, a telephone but, unfortunately, the local exchange closed down for lunch between twelve o'clock and two. However, she would be delighted if the Captain would have lunch with the family and then get in touch with the telephone exchange. The Captain was also delighted especially when his eyes rested upon the petite and attractive daughter of the Countess. He married her! This was, of course, after the usual long-drawn-out preliminaries. When the war finished Mr Baseden returned to his peace-time engineering employment which involved travelling about the countries of Europe. The family was living in Paris when a little girl, whom they christened Yvonne, was born in 1923.

She grew into a lithe, sports-loving girl as she travelled from country to country with her parents. She attended schools in Poland, Belgium, Holland, Italy and Spain and apart from her fluent French and English picked up a good smattering of several European languages. She was a gentle girl whom her father urged to attend physical training and gymnastic classes. She became a fair tumbler, sailed a lot, won several cups for her skill on the ice and was a good shot.

In 1937 her parents settled in London and Yvonne became a boarder at the Convent school of St Mary's in Tottenham, North London. She was an obedient and charming pupil but not exactly a genius at studies. When she was sixteen she left the convent and liking the out-door life took employment on an apple-farm in Bedfordshire.

When her parents moved to Southampton in 1939 she went to live with them again and took a job as a bilingual shorthand-typist in a local engineering firm. When she became eighteen she dropped everything else and joined the ranks of the Royal Air Force. She was motivated by her equally-divided love for two countries—England and France. She had wept bitterly when she heard on the wireless that France had capitulated to the Germans. From her mother she had inherited a great love for France and had lived long enough in that country to know it and its people well; likewise through her father and her domicile she had come to regard England and its people with affection and respect.

On the appointed day, an only slightly interested Yvonne presented herself at the door of the Ministry of Pensions in London and showed her letter to the commissionaire. He handed her over to a messenger who led her through several corridors to a drab-looking door in a distant corner of the establishment. The messenger knocked and when a voice answered, 'Come in', he opened the door, ushered her in, did not enter himself and closed the door behind her. Yvonne found herself in a barely furnished room—there was but one table and two chairs. A middle aged, kindly looking man sat at the table. He stood up, shook hands with her and pointed to the vacant chair. When she sat down he opened a folder and said —'Miss Baseden, you were born in the Rue Violet in Paris in 1923,' and Yvonne was thinking that this was something to do with pensions. But then he told her in detail the story of her life to date and he also knew all there was to know about her family. He knew the work she was doing at the time and he was sure that it was important and very useful, but he said, as he folded his hands across the folder, 'There is other very important work that you could be doing—would you care to return to France now and help the French Resistance in its fight against the German forces?' The idea coming out of the blue made her suddenly feel breathless and then exhilarated —'Yes,' she said, 'I would love to.'

And then he explained about the work and the training for it, the rigours she would face. Even the training would be a major task and that would lead to service 'in the field'. He carefully explained the risks and the probable hardships and he was eloquent about her fate if she fell into enemy hands—he seemed now almost to be trying to dissuade her. But she repeated, 'Yes. I would love to go.'

When she returned to her unit that evening she was in a quandary. She could not tell her friends why she would soon be leaving them, nor where she was going and she was unwilling to tell them direct lies. She compromised with a nearly-true story of changing her department and having a holiday in between. She had a similar problem with her father and he, whatever he may have guessed, did not press her.

A few days after her interview she was instructed to leave her unit and report to an address in London. Swiftly—and not exactly to her taste—she found herself an Officer in the First Aid Nursing Yeomanry. She had a vague knowledge of the corps—it was known as the F.A.N.Y.s—and she had a dim idea that it provided young ladies to drive generals and other high-ranking officers from their offices to clubs and to their homes in the country. In fact the F.A.N.Y.s were a very important adjunct to SOE and provided an excellent cover for many of the firm's activities.

The remote mountains, moors and lochs of Scotland were excellent training grounds for troops—especially the special units like the Commandos, Special Air Service and Special Boat section. Strangers were sparse on the ground there and unauthorized persons could not go undetected for long. A few days after she had enrolled in the F.A.N.Y.s Yvonne was posted to a commando training unit in that area.

She discovered that the instructors had little regard for the sex of their pupils—no exceptions and no allowances were made. She was lucky, her physical training and gym practice stood her in good stead now and she was well up with the leaders in the rigorous field training, rock-climbing and back-breaking treks through the heather, loaded down with weapons and explosives. She learned to use the rifle, sten-gun and bren gun; to throw hand grenades; to mix and detonate plastic explosive and to use a pistol in a swift and efficient manner. She was given elementary training in the use of a wireless transmitter. She came through the training well and gave every satisfaction in the frequent interviews which went on through every stage of the training. Her efficiency, aptitude and temperament marked her out at this stage for the most dangerous job of all—that of becoming a wireless operator in the field.

After she had passed out from Scotland she was sent for parachute training to Ringway aerodrome near Manchester where, as we have seen, she completed five drops and had some little difficulty because of her light weight. At her next interview with SOE executives she was told that they felt she would be suitable to become a wireless-operator and again the risks and dangers of that particular occupation were spelt out to her. She accepted and began five tedious months of training in morse, codes, maintenance of the cumbersome transmitting and receiving sets and continuous practice until she reached the necessary speeds of transmission and receiving. Speed and accuracy were vital 'in the field' when the success of operations and often lives were dependent on the skill of the W.T. operator.

When she had reached the required standard she was sent with her set to a town in the north of England to carry out a practical exercise. She had never been in the town before, she had to obtain digs, and operate her set from her location avoiding detection from our own security forces who would be searching for her and also from our own wireless detection services. She had certain information to transmit and she knew that she must send it so quickly that the wireless-detection vans would not have time to get a 'fix' on the location.

Yvonne found a room in a boarding-house and at the appointed hour rigged an aerial from the curtain hooks and safely dispatched the message. She was not detected. She left the wireless school a fully-fledged wireless operator and went for the last part of her training to a 'safe' house in the south of England. This was one of many establishments maintained by the Firm. Usually these houses were situated in their own grounds in the country and were closely guarded. They were run by selected members of the F.A.N.Y.s acting as cooks, house-maids and house-keepers.

The final course was on security. The fully trained and approved student—often called 'the bod'—would shortly become a member of the civilian population of France, liable to be questioned by the German security authorities at any moment of the day or night and in any place from the village square to the trespassed privacy of the bedroom. It was essential, therefore, that each person was well abreast of prevailing conditions as well as being confident and well versed in his, or her, own cover story. At this stage instructors gave detailed descriptions of the ration-books, passes and permits that the agents would carry with them in the field. They were shown the uniforms and the badges of rank of the several different sections of the German forces and security services, the police and the Milice—a militia police force of treacherous French men and women who gave their allegiance to the Germans. They were, if possible, even more vicious and feared than their masters and had a more intimate knowledge of France and its people.

The agents were told about the feelings of the French people—whom they could place most trust in and of whom to be wary. Not everybody in France was a member of the French Resistance; indeed, as was to be expected in such circumstances a proportion of the population were pro-German. The mass of the people whilst supporting the resistance passively had to live ordinary law-abiding lives trying to avoid becoming involved in the new and awful 'terror'. The innocent population suffered a great deal from the reprisals of the German forces to the aggressive violence of the Resistance, nor were they ever safe from the sudden whims and fancies of the ruthless and often sadistic invaders.

The agents were told what to expect if they fell into the hands of the Germans—they were given frighteningly realistic mock-ups of Gestapo questioning methods. They would be roughly woken up at some time during the night and kicked and pushed whilst still drowsy in front of dazzling lights. 'Gestapo' officials in genuine uniforms would then shout and rave at them in the authentic fashion—some of the questioners indeed knew the correct drill because they themselves had experienced questioning by Gestapo officers. After the war some of the agents who had been captured confirmed that this mock-up had served a useful purpose.

Her security course finished, Yvonne returned to London to report to the SOE Headquarters which were situated in Baker Street—within a stone's throw of the legendary home of Sherlock Holmes. Here she was introduced to a brilliant young French officer, Gonzagues de St Genies; he was to be her commander in the field. Their task was to set up a new resistance group in the French province of the Jura, a province on the borders of Switzerland. They were told what identities to assume in the field—Yvonne became Mademoiselle Yvonne Bernier and reverted to her old pre-war job of shorthand-typist secretary—and were issued with papers, passes and ration books in their new names. They were also told their 'cover' stories. They were given two weeks to absorb and rehearse their new identities, learn their cover stories and familiarize themselves with the district to which they had been posted.

Gonzagues had fought with the French forces and had been captured and sent to Germany. Determined to be free to continue the fight he had made several unsuccessful attempts to get away—eventually he broke his arm with an axe and was repatriated. He then set out on the long and hazardous escape route to England which he reached in 1943 and immediately volunteered for, and was accepted and trained for service with the Resistance. Their final interview was a searching interrogation of their cover stories which they passed with flying colours and they were told to hold themselves in immediate readiness for a flight to France. A few nights afterwards they were driven to an aerodrome in the south of England. They were asked to fire a few test shots from their pistols and were then led across the darkened tarmac to their aircraft.

The plane flew high across the coast of France to avoid the flak from the German ack-ack defences and then swooped towards the dropping zone in the south of France. As the pilot approached he saw an aircraft about to take off from an airfield and he looked in vain for the signals from the ground to tell him that the 'reception committee' was awaiting him. He had no alternative but to return to England. It was a miserable anti-climax for the two 'bods' sitting in their parachutes near the exit awaiting the signal to jump.

Two nights later they set out again, everything went smoothly and they landed safely.

Yvonne, now 'Odette' and Gonzagues, now 'Lucien' sat in the farmer's kitchen drinking ersatz coffee as the leader of the reception group went through the mail which had just been dropped. He was a British officer who had earned a legendary reputation in the service of the Resistance. His field name was Hilaire. He was George Starr who had started the war as an officer's batman and finished it as Lieutenant-Colonel Starr DSO, MC, Legion of Honour. He had been 'in the field' since 1942 and had won golden opinions in London and France for his energy, efficiency, daring and success.

In the mail was a letter from his wife with recent pictures of the children and herself. After they had been passed around the party broke up. Lucien went off by himself, he had some messages from London to deliver. Yvonne was given a bicycle and she went with Hilaire on her first journey through the dark lanes of France to the house which he was using at the time as his headquarters. There she met two other young ladies from Britain—Yvonne Cormeau, another wireless operator, and also an ex-officer of the Women's Auxiliary Air Force. The third girl was also an ex-Waaf, Anne-Marie Walters who was both a wireless operator and courier for Hilaire. The three of them had plenty to talk about, Yvonne brought fresh news from London and they had a great deal to tell her about life, and how to live it, as a secret agent in German-occupied France. It was but a brief respite for Yvonne because a messenger arrived from Lucien within a couple of days to tell her to pack up her wireless transmitter set and join him for the journey across France to the Jura.

Now she saw at first hand all that she had been told to expect in her training. France was in a sorry state. The people were near starved, downtrodden and frightened. British and American aircraft were, at this time, continually bombing and strafing railway stations, factories, and electrical installations. Transport and communications were disrupted by the air-raids as well as by the fighters of the Resistance—the Germans too were frightened and more dangerous. Millions of French people had been transported to factories and concentration camps in Germany. Every fit man and woman lived in fear of being apprehended and deported to help the German war effort. Thousands of young people had left their homes and were living with the Maquis in remote country areas. The Allies were stepping up the offensive in preparation for the climax which was to be D-day—the landing of the allied armies.

Lucien and Yvonne travelled by trains for four days across France—time and again there were delays—the Resistance had blown up the lines or the British had bombed sidings or bridges. Railway stations and trains were packed with nervous French people and nervous and suspicious German troops and security services. Yvonne had her cumbersome and dangerous luggage with her. There were unexpected German control points when their passes and forged travel permits were scrutinized.

In crowded compartments she had to be careful what she said to her travelling companions, often there were German soldiers in the carriage or standing in the corridors. Once she travelled in a carriage with four German officers—she concentrated on believing in her new identity and was worried about what she might say in her sleep—she was a shorthand typist travelling on legitimate business to the sombrely-named town of Dole. She hoped she did not look as English as she felt.

She reached Dole safely and was re-united with Lucien who had travelled separately on the train. She had successfully come through her first test as a secret agent. At Dole a safe house had been prepared for them and there was immediate work for her. Lucien travelled about daily meeting members of the group, finding out what was needed, teaching new recruits how to use guns and explosives. He and Yvonne also, during the daylight hours, were scanning the countryside for suitable dropping zones—the arms and ammunition would soon start arriving. They marked the vital spots in the area as well—the railway stations, the sidings, the signal boxes and the electrical supply depots.

Every night Yvonne sat at her transmitting set sending the messages she had been handed, to London. She had to alter her transmitting spots frequently because the German direction-finding vans were soon on her trail. Her messages had to be transmitted swiftly so that they did not have time to get a 'fix' on her. Every night also she had to listen to the radio programmes from London—every night the BBC broadcast series of innocent sounding phrases which were coded instructions and information to the several resistance groups all over France. A message such as 'Henri has a boil on his neck' might mean 'arms and supplies will be dropped to you at 15.30 hours.'

All through the months of April and May the work went on at an ever-increasing pace. There was little time for rest now —day and night the work went on and day and night also the Germans were working, seeking out the operator and the group which they knew were in their midst. Some nights she would transmit from the corner of a field, other times from a barn, or the shelter of a hay-rick. Frequently after transmitting she would join a reception committee and await the arrival of aircraft which would drop parachute containers crammed with weapons of war. As the aircraft zoomed away to Britain the group would frantically recover the containers and bury them nearby or take them to a safe place before daybreak.

With June came a further increase in the pace—the Resistance did not know for sure but they believed that the invasion was very near. During June the night sky over France was noisy with the sound of British aircraft dropping supplies—and the ranks of the Resistance were growing day by day. London was being asked for more and more.

One night instructions came that Lucien was to isolate the town of Dole—every railway line was to be blocked or blown, every telephone and telegraph line to be put out of action—then came the messages and the realization that it was the invasion—it was 6th June 1944. But Normandy where the allies had landed was a long way from the Jura. That night Lucien's group worked hard and in the morning Dole had been completely isolated—no one entered or left it that day and the only lines of communication were through the German field radio and Yvonne's transmitter.

That night was the culmination of four hard years of preparation. As the troops were landing in Normandy the Resistance all over France was carrying out the work it had been preparing for. It was made impossible for the Germans to send reinforcements to their hard-pressed forces near the coast. The resistance did the work of many army divisions—SOE had proved itself. But the conflict was far from over—indeed, for most of France the position became more desperate. The Resistance had shown its strength and its efficiency—the Germans became more ruthless now they knew they were fighting for survival.

The invasion had also the effect of sending more and more of the civilian population to join the ranks of the Maquis and the other resistance groups and it became more urgent to increase the supply of weapons. London now hard-pressed for more and more supplies had a new and exciting idea—an enormous daylight drop of hundreds of containers from a fleet of giant American aircraft—the Flying Fortresses!

At the time Lucien and Yvonne were using a cheese depot standing in its own grounds as headquarters. It was a rambling old house which had once been an orphanage and nobody lived there except the nightwatchman and his wife, Monsieur and Madame Mayer who were trusted members of the Resistance.

Large Gruyère cheeses were stored in the basement, the first floor was used as a cheese factory and the Mayers lived on the first floor. The floor above was a high-lofted apartment which could only be reached by walking through the flat. It was a rambling, picturesque place permeated with the pleasant aroma of ripening cheeses.

Never before had a daylight arms drop been considered and it required the most detailed planning and preparation. Thirty-six Flying Fortresses were to be used and nearly five hundred containers dropped. Lucien had to find the dropping ground. He chose one which was contained in a triangle of roads so that the approaches to it could be covered by the Maquis. He arranged eight hundred to be alerted and armed, transport to remove the containers had to be organized—he found twenty-seven vehicles. Yvonne was frantically busy sending and receiving messages—Sunday morning 26th June was chosen for the operation. She was the vital link between the forces waiting on the ground and the Headquarters staff in London who had to liaise with the American airforce, the supply depots, fighter squadrons and the transport services. An enormous risk was involved—for the first time in the Jura the organized forces of the Maquis would surface as a fighting, guarding force.

As it was a daylight operation the usual recognition system from the ground was replaced by what was known as an S-Phone. This was a transmitting and receiving set by which an operator on the ground could talk directly to an aircraft. Yvonne was to operate the S-Phone, guiding the aircraft to the dropping zone and keeping them in touch with conditions in the area. After nights of frenzied preparation at Dole and in London the operation was declared on.

That Sunday morning people on their way to Church services were amazed to see armed members of the Maquis patrolling the roads and guarding entrenched points overlooking the road. The ruffianly-looking men were each wearing an armlet bearing the cross of Lorraine—the Resistance symbol.

Yvonne had been at her post for the previous twenty-four hours and was seated near the dropping field guarded by members of the Maquis. She had an hourly schedule to keep with London—they needed to know that conditions for dropping continued to remain good and that the Germans had not been alerted. If the entire consignment of arms fell into German hands it would have been an enormous loss and a dreadful blow to the Resistance prestige. Scouts and dispatch riders patrolled the field and the near-by area and reported to Yvonne every half hour.

At 8 a.m. she made her first contact with the aircraft as they crossed the English channel and sent them her O.K. messages every ten minutes. As 9 o'clock approached excitement on the ground reached fever pitch—soon the noise of the approaching armada was heard and Yvonne was in direct-speech contact with the Commander, the air raid warnings were sounded in Dole and the Germans, as they usually did, 'went to ground' leaving the whole operation to proceed unhampered.

When the aircraft were over the ground she gave the final, 'all right', message and leaving her set ran on to the field. The sky was filled with descending containers, men were rushing about avoiding them as they grabbed the ones that had landed and manhandled them to the waiting vehicles. Everybody was excited and helping, the din was terrific and the activity enormous. Soon the last container had been dropped, she hurried back to the set and dashed off the O.K. followed by the V. signal.

When everything had been collected she joined Lucien and they went with the convoy of arms to a rendezvous in the forest. That afternoon was spent distributing the arms to the Maquis and in the evening after refreshments she shared a tent with ten of the leaders. Next morning with Lucien she returned to the cheese factory. They were to have a celebration lunch there with some of their colleagues—everything had been wonderfully successful.

At midday they sat down to the excellent meal prepared by Madame Mayer—the only slight fly in the ointment was that the young lad who was driving a cart of logs to the house had not yet arrived. Yvonne's wireless set and some weapons were hidden under the logs.

At one o'clock Madame's sharp ears picked up the sound of a motor cycle and she went to the window to look out. 'Hurry,' she called out, 'It's the Germans!' Two German motor-cyclists followed by two car-loads of soldiers were coming down the drive from the road.

The probability of raids by the Germans had been foreseen and everybody knew where they had to hide in the house. They quickly dispersed, but there was not enough time to completely clear up the remains of the meal. The Germans came in to find Madame Mayer washing up. Her friends had been in for lunch she told them, but had left. The Germans were not impressed. They knew something now about the giant dropping operation of yesterday. They had found the lad driving the cart full of logs—they searched it and found the wireless set and the weapons. The lad was not helpful, but they had beaten him unmercifully, his face was pulped and one of his eyes was badly damaged. All he had eventually admitted was that he was on his way to the Mayer's house. The Germans made a search of the house, but found nothing. Madame thought they were about to leave when two more car-loads arrived. This time there were high-ranking officers and Gestapo officials.

Another and more detailed search was made and still they found nothing suspicious. Madame become hopeful again, but then the water in the pipes made a gurgling noise—it was nothing unusual, it often made that noise, but it aroused the suspicions of the Germans. Another and a more drastic search was ordered. The Germans had been in the house for two hours by now and neither Yvonne nor any of her companions had made the slightest sound. She had dropped down into an opening left in a pile of wooden posts, she was squeezed there, uncomfortable, but quiet. She could hear the Germans talking and the sound of their boots as they walked about. She was in the loft over the Mayers' living quarters. The soldiers came into the loft and began to move the huge pile of wooden posts from one side of the loft to the other. It was a long and strenuous task—then they found one of the men. They knocked him to the floor and one of them guarded him as the work went on. Three more were found and similarly treated. Then a soldier who had been standing directly above where Yvonne was hiding shone a torch down and saw her. He fired a shot from his rifle. It missed her. She put her arms up to be pulled out, but he ignored them and catching her by the hair dragged her up. He crashed his fist into her face, knocked her out and threw her on the floor.

Now the Germans started firing shots through the floor-boards and downstairs blood began to seep through the ceiling. They tore up the floor-boards and dragged men out, some of them were dead, others wounded. Yvonne recovered consciousness to see the bodies of the dead and wounded being thrown on the floor—she saw Lucien and he was dead. A bullet had passed through his head. They found everybody except Monsieur Mayer. He was hidden deep amongst his cheeses. The walking prisoners were handcuffed together and pushed into the yard, the wounded were dragged out and laid on the ground. It was now nine o'clock in the evening, their misery and feelings of helplessness were heightened by a severe summer storm of driving rain and vivid lightning which now broke.

As well as the motor cars there were now three horse-drawn supply wagons in the yard, driven and guarded by Russian soldiers who had been captured on the Eastern front and were now working for the Germans. Yvonne was pushed into one of the supply carts. The dead and wounded were thrown into the other and the miserable party set out for the German military barracks in Dole. Lucien was dead and the group shattered. The one bright note was that, as far as she could tell Mr Mayer had not been caught. He could warn the rest of the group who would now have to disperse—somebody would get word back to London. The arms were safe and the work could continue.

At the barracks Yvonne and Mrs Mayer were thrown into a cell with a strange woman whom they suspected of being a stoolpigeon for the Germans. The eight men they had captured were locked in another small cell. Those who had been wounded were untreated, the body of Lucien was thrown in with them. Madame Mayer who had so bravely stood the rigours of the day now broke down completely. She became demented with worry and tried to kill herself by hitting her head against the cell walls. Yvonne tried to restrain her, but did not have the strength and her cries for help went unanswered. At midday next day they were given something to eat, afterwards they were left alone, except for meal breaks, for three days. Once they were taken out for brief questioning about their identities—Yvonne gave her cover story and at the time it seemed to satisfy them. A couple of days afterwards she was called out again. So was the lad who had driven the cartload of logs and who had been badly beaten. They were taken to Dijon which was the operational centre for the Germans in that part of France. On arrival at the detention centre they were both questioned in a reasonable manner by some junior members of the Gestapo who decided that they should be put back in their cells to await the arrival of more senior members of that organization.

Two days later Yvonne's cell door was thrown open and two men in civilian clothes entered. Brusquely they pushed her into a car and drove to their own headquarters which was a detached and closely guarded building surrounded by sentry boxes and barbed wire. They took her to an office and began their questioning politely and non-committally. She repeated her well-learnt cover story—that she was a local shorthand-typist who had become involved with some members of the Resistance.

When they decided to have their lunch they handcuffed her to a radiator and left her alone and without food to ponder her circumstances. She wondered when they would start the 'rough stuff'—she had no illusions about the immediate future. She derived some comfort from the fact that there had been plenty of time for Lucien's group to have dispersed and the arms must be safe. She knew too that she could not really give away much that was of vital value, the agents had been told during training that they should try hard not to reveal anything during the first twenty-four hours of capture. If they could hold out for that time it would give the other members of the group time to disperse, to change their codes and their meeting-places and to let London know what had happened. Security within the resistance had always been orientated towards no one member knowing too much about what was happening in other groups, or even in their own group. This meant that they could not, under torture, give too much away.

When the Gestapo couple returned after lunch their mood and their method changed. Now they were hostile, aggressive and contemptuous, they tore her cover story to pieces and confronted her with conflicting statements from the other prisoners whom they had questioned. They threatened her with immediate and intense penalties if she did not tell the truth.

She continued to deny everything and acted as stupidly as she could; she admitted nothing. They became impatient, cuffed her, pushed her down the stairs and threw her into a filthy damp underground cell where there was no furniture except a few planks to serve as a bed. They slammed the door, switched the light off from the outside and went away.

She was there in the pitch darkness without food or water for three days. She heard a church clock striking the hours and sometimes people in other cells screaming as they were being beaten. Shivering, hungry and confused she fell into a dreadful state of misery and hopelessness. She scrambled about on her hands and knees and found a bottle in the corner of the cell. She threw it hard against the wall and was terrified by the noise it made—but nobody came. She chose a fragment of the glass and stabbed at her wrist trying to cut a vein—but she could not find the same place twice in the dark and her hands were weak and trembling—the pain and faintness forced her to give up. Some time later she found a piece of rag and tying it about her throat tried to strangle herself, but her arms were too weak and when she fainted the knot relaxed. Covered in vermin and having lost all awareness of time or place she lay semi-conscious on the planks.

Then the cell was flooded with light and the same two men appeared and motioned her to get out and up the stairs. They stood watching as she dragged herself up and into their office. They spoke to her in English but she was not tricked and she pretended not to understand. But now they had new evidence that she was a British agent; they knew her code name and that she was a trained wireless operator; now they shouted at her for information. She no longer denied it, she told them a long, rambling and untrue story which seemed to give them some satisfaction. Most of all they wanted to know the name of the British aerodrome from which she had flown to France. She did not, in fact, know its name—but they would not believe her. One of them pushed her against the wall and standing on her bare toes swayed himself back and forwards—she was semi-conscious and it struck her as being funny and quite ridiculous; she was past feeling any more pain.

They pushed her down to the cell again and one of them took out his pistol and fired it at her feet. It missed but threw up fragments of stone and dust. Then he pointed it at her head and demanded to know the name—she thought it was now all over. He fired again but only to miss her. They turned their backs and left her in the darkness again. They had finished with her and a few hours later she was taken back to the other prison and given food and drink. She remained in a cell there until the end of August.

The allied advance had by now penetrated into the heart of France and late in August Paris was surrendered by the Germans. The following day all the prisoners in Dijon including Yvonne and Mrs Mayer were sent to Germany.

On the way they stopped for a short while at the men's camp at Saarbrucken where Yvonne saw for the first time the unbelievable horrors of a German concentration camp. There were living skeletons with shaven heads, crawling in the hot sun. Others were being forced to run in circles until they dropped and then kicked to their feet again. She met some girls there who had been captured in Paris—including another F.A.N.Y. officer and agent—Lilian Rolfe.

One morning Yvonne, and a batch of seventy women, were marched to the station and packed into an enclosed cattle truck. The doors were locked and the train stood for hours in the boiling sun. It pulled out in the evening and began a nightmare three-day journey. Once a day they were given a bowl of soup, but never water. On the fourth day the train stopped at

Ravensbruck railway station, the doors were opened and hundreds of miserable and distressed creatures were spewed out. There was a reception committee awaiting them. Groups of smartly dressed Aufscherinnen—the women guards of Ravensbruck—were in groups laughing and talking. They had dogs with them and they carried whips. The prisoners were marched through two miles of beautiful countryside and pine woods which perfumed the air. The hedgerows were bright with summer flowers—the only sounds were of shuffling feet, barked orders from the women-guards and, occasionally, the crack of a wielded whip.

Ravensbruck was the most notorious of the women's concentration camps. 110,000 unfortunate women passed through its entrance gates—only 12,000 of whom survived. Yvonne experienced its indescribable horror for eight months—from early September 1944 until 26th April 1945. Her indelibly tattooed number was 62,947. It was a place of dead and dying women, of fear, terror and starvation.

Every morning at 4.30 a.m. a ghastly parade of the inmates began. Rows of suffering women stood in silent ranks in all weathers for over two hours. Everyone capable of standing had to attend—children and dying women. About seven o'clock groups of them were marched to work—coal heaving, potato picking, unloading railway carriages, felling trees. They worked till 7 p.m. and were given a twenty-minute break at midday and issued with a bowl of soup—carrot in summer, cabbage in autumn and mangel-wurzel in the winter. After work they drew a piece of bread and a slice of some kind of sausage. January was a bitter month, there was no water because the pipes had frozen, dysentry raged and rations were cut. Demented women fought each other for scraps of dirt to eat, the death rate rocketed and the smoke stacks of the crematoriums belched forth black smoke day and night.

But the inmates were not dying quickly enough so it was decided to kill them—three hundred of the most dangerous prisoners were shot and gas chambers were installed to quicken the pace. In February and March 'selection' was introduced. An officer walked down the ranks pointing to prisoners who should be exterminated—literally now the odour of the dead and dying permeated the camp. Yvonne saw terrified women pick dirt from the ground and rub it on their heads to disguise grey hairs. The old and the weakest were the first to go. She was herself feeble and ailing and wondered when it would be her turn. The allies were now in Germany itself and the inmates guessed that the Germans wanted to hide the evidence of the 'camps' before the troops arrived. Their fears were confirmed when the machine guns on the walls were turned inwards and drums of oil were brought into the compounds.

But, miraculously, Red Cross parties arrived and took some of the prisoners away. In April the Swedish Red Cross party insisted on removing all the British prisoners they could find alive—in spite of the Commandant's protests—and Yvonne was in the party. Soon she had the comfort of an ambulance and expert care. Then by car, train, boat and aircraft she passed through Germany, Switzerland, Sweden and Scotland. She arrived in London one fine summer's day—Whit Sunday 20th May 1945. She had to enter hospital for a serious operation on her lungs and then after some months of convalescence she rejoined the Women's Auxiliary Air Force. She was posted to her old unit, the Bombing Survey Unit and quietly resumed the duties which SOE had interrupted.

2

WHYS AND WHEREFORES

Yvonne was one of fifty women who were infiltrated into France by Special Operations Executive between 1942 and 1944. Each of them knew well what the risks were and were made fully aware of the conditions under which they would work. If anything, conditions turned out to be worse than even the most pessimistic of the instructors had envisaged but there was not one case of a woman agent betraying her trust nor of flinching from her duty in the face of the worst that the callous and, eventually, panic-stricken enemy could do.

As well as the 39 women, 430 men were sent into the field by the French Section. Of the total sent, 375 survived, many of them wounded or broken by the dreadful conditions of captivity in German prisons and concentration camps. Casualties were, therefore, about 25 per cent—a very high rate but not, in fact, as high as the authorities expected. Remember that each agent was working actively and aggressively in the midst of a nervous population infiltrated and surrounded by shrewd and suspicious enemy forces. Of the 39 women who went, 13 died, 12 of these were killed by the Germans and twenty-two year old Muriel Byck, a little Jewish girl, died of meningitis in the field in May 1944. Three of the girls who returned survived German concentration camps. High the casualty rate certainly was, but it was low in proportion to the results that the section achieved.

General Eisenhower, the Supreme Commander, wrote in May 1945—'I consider that the disruption of enemy rail communications, the harassing of German road moves and the continual and increasing strain placed on the German war economy and internal security services throughout occupied Europe by the organized forces of resistance played a very considerable part in our complete and final victory'.

In September 1941 the French Section was started and Colonel Maurice Buckmaster was appointed its Commanding Officer. His headquarters were in offices at Baker Street, London, which had previously been occupied by Marks and Spencer, the chain store people.

Before the war Colonel Buckmaster had been manager of the French company of Ford Motors. He joined the army on the outbreak of war and fought with the British Expeditionary Force before the fall of France—he had been mentioned in despatches. He was one of the last men to leave Dunkirk with the remnants of the British army in 1940.

Amongst his small but highly efficient Headquarter's staff was a remarkable woman who carried RAF Squadron Officer rank named Vera Wilkins. A brilliant woman with an analytical mind and extraordinary powers of perception, she possessed—and still possesses—a great humanity and kindliness. She, more than anybody, knew all there was to know about the women agents who left Britain to work in occupied France. She saw them off on their moonlight departures and followed their fortunes in the field. She, as well as Colonel Buckmaster, was forbidden to go into the field themselves because they knew too much of the workings of Special Operations Executive and their superiors were unwilling to risk either of them falling into enemy hands. Vera was described as 'the real brain of the French Section' and 'the most powerful personality in SOE' by knowledgeable leaders, and I, having met many of the agents, know what they think about her. They regard her with a kind of respectful awe tempered with gratitude and affection.

Amongst her many duties at SOE was that of ensuring that the agents went into the field properly prepared. Even the slightest details were vitally important. It was Vera who checked that the clothing, buttons and threads were correct according to prevailing French conditions. She supplied the right documentary evidence and the precise conditions prevailing in the area to which the agent was going. She saw to it that nothing in the agent's handbag was incongruous, for it could awaken the suspicions of a keen Gestapo man. Her agile mind and encyclopaedic memory stored and sorted each scrap of information which reached England from France—and she carefully saved every scrap of paper as well—empty cigarette packets, theatre tickets and bus tickets that came from France. They went back to lend credibility to the contents of the girls' handbags and pockets.

She absorbed all she could discover about working conditions, travel, food, rationing and black-marketeering,—and the commonest and most detailed information about living conditions. She found 'family snapshots', visiting cards, and letters from friends that could be included in the agent's effects. She ensured that the dressmaker's tabs on coats and skirts were authentic. She spent a few days with each girl who left—before their departure—in order to help her eradicate any personal habit or idiosyncrasy which might give her away to a quick-witted Frenchman or German. She watched them at table, and saw how they used their knives and forks, condiments and sauces and at the tea-table. The French, for example, do not put the milk in the tea-cup first—they add it to the tea in the cup. And on the final drive from London to the airfield Vera would be there to probe gently in case the girl had any other wishes, personal messages to pass on, or worries.

She continued her interest when the agent was in the field. Many of them had close relatives, children, wives, husbands or parents about whom they were concerned. The highly confidential nature of the work made it difficult but Vera founded a kind of information service by which personal news was passed to the agents. It helped them to relax and stop worrying. Many of them called her 'The Guardian Angel'.

The very idea of recruiting women for such perilous work in German-occupied France was, at first, a sensational and revolutionary one. I asked Vera about it and she said, 'I well remember the heated discussions which took place when the idea was first put forward. It was the beginning of 1942, and it was vital to establish regular communications with London and internally between an organizer and his various groups. Wireless operators and couriers were wanted, and women were suited to the job, as they could move about more freely in occupied territory. Men were more suspect. Eventually, of course, several women couriers were called upon to fill a man's place after a sudden arrest, and the women wireless operators did the same work as the men.

'I knew them all fairly well, and saw them at different stages from the time they joined. Many I accompanied down to the aerodrome when they went off. What I admired so much was not their courage, which I am afraid one took for granted, but their charming, disarming simplicity. No display of temperament, no bravado. Yet they might have been excused a little show of pride. Today, the greater number are happy wives and mothers, and the others have settled into different everyday jobs. These women were not seeking adventure and glamour, but rather to help personally and without rancour towards carrying the war to a successful finish'.

It was, indeed, safer and easier—comparatively speaking—for women to move about in France at that time. Able-bodied men of military age were liable to be seized by the Germans and deported to work in German factories. Thousands of such men were 'on the run' from their homes living with the Maquis in remote forests and moors to avoid being so conscripted.

It was, however, essential for the British officers organizing the resistance to send messages to members of their groups and for this work couriers were essential. It was also necessary to move about the country in the day-time looking for likely places for parachute drops of supplies and arms, and suitable landing grounds were also needed where aircraft from Britain could touch down. So couriers, particularly women couriers had plenty of urgent and vital work to do.

It would have been almost useless for the Resistance groups and officers to exist without being in constant touch with Headquarters in London—for this work wireless operators were needed. Accurate information was required about the disposal of enemy forces, the location of factories and the nature of the work being done in them—up-to-date reports about communications and the uses to which they were being put.

Information from the field was passed on by SOE to the Royal Air Force and acting on this information forces of bombers would visit the area to put vital plants and marshalling yards and other important strategic places out of action. Wrong or out-of-date information might mean wasting the bombers on sterile trips such as demolishing a factory which had switched to making dolls' prams.

For the wireless operator it was a very hazardous and onerous life. She had to have her heavy and difficult-to-disguise transmitting set which weighed about thirty pounds with her wherever she went. If she was discovered with one she was immediately condemned as a British agent. She was obliged to stick closely to a regular routine of listening to and sending messages to London. Each had regular, scheduled times for this when her opposite number in Britain was waiting to receive or send.

In the darkness and in all weathers she might have to stand by her set in wild and remote places. Usually she rigged up seventy feet of aerial wire and operated from safe houses, barns or other innocent-looking buildings and before and after her schedule had to wrestle with the complicated job of coding and decoding the messages. The moment the set went 'on the air' the risks were increased a thousand-fold. The German direction-finder services—the 'D-Effers'—would usually pick them up immediately and try desperately to obtain a true 'fix' on their location. The longer the operator was broadcasting the more chance they had, and if the signals always came from the same location it gave the 'D-Effers' a good clue.

The Germans had several successes. One British girl—Yolande Beekman—a wireless operator and a WAAF officer who was obliged to send long signals from the same location for a long period, was captured by the 'D-Effers.' After the usual brutal questioning and ill-treatment they shot her through the back of the neck in Dachau concentration camp in 1944. Two other girls captured by similar methods were Noor Inayat Khan, a half-Indian girl and ex-WAAF, who was also executed by the Germans and awarded a posthumous George Cross, and Eileen Nearne, whose sister Jacqueline was a courier. Eileen, like Yvonne Baseden and Odette Churchill, managed to survive the German concentration camps.

None of the girls knew anything about the finer points of wireless telegraphy before they joined. It was during their training that some special aptitude on their part was noticed by the instructors and mentioned in their reports. The fact that they accepted the task did not excuse them from the full rigours of SOE training—it meant one extra and very difficult course. Neither were activities in the field restricted to wireless-telegraphy. When available they acted as couriers and showed the members of the resistance how to use the sten-guns and other small arms that were being supplied by the British. They lectured on hand-grenades and how to throw them and they passed on as much as they could of the information they had picked up during their training.

Plastic explosive (PE) was a weapon which did an enormous amount of damage in France. It was a British invention, and ideal for guerrilla warfare. It resembled plasticine and could be moulded easily into shapes to fill all kinds of holes and corners. It was a very 'safe' explosive which would not go off if it was burnt or hit by a bullet. One man who even ate some in mistake for chocolate suffered no ill-effects. The girls showed their pupils how to and where to place it on railway-lines, rolling stock, and bridges to achieve best results.

The reactions of the girls to the strict and sometimes even brutal training were mixed: some of them enjoyed it very much, others found it unpleasant and boring, others resented the physical effort it required. Such a one was Nancy Wake, an attractive rumbustious Australian girl. She also cheated cheerfully in her tests and got through them all. Nancy, whose well-shaped bosom at the end of hostilities boasted more medals and decorations than any of the other girls, shamefully pleaded feminine weakness in order to avoid early morning physical training on cold mornings. She cut corners on her cross-country runs and had a flaming row with a superior officer who so much resented her colourful and 'ungentlemanly' abuse that she was actually banished from the organization—but wiser counsels prevailed and she was readmitted. That officer was lucky that their disagreement did not lead to violence or he might have ended up dead like the German sentry she tackled with her bare hands a few months afterwards.

Like most of the girls Nancy came into touch with the organization through the merest accident. She spotted a man reading an English book in a French bar, her curiosity was aroused and she discovered that he was a captured British officer on parole—she eventually helped him to escape and thus came to the notice of SOE.

Peggy Smith, a diminutive English girl who had been invalided out of the WAAFs, joined because she met a man with a French book in an English bar in the Strand in London. He dropped it accidentally and she picked it up and handed it to him—as she did she read the title of the book aloud. 'You have a very good French accent,' he said. As a result she found herself parachuting to French soil a few short months afterwards. He happened to be one of the senior officers of the organization!

Lise de Baissac who completed two outstandingly successful missions in the field was invited to join the organization because her brother recommended her. Advancing American troops did not believe their eyes when they overran a French village after D-day to find Lise dressed in her neat F.A.N.Y. uniform awaiting them.

Jacqueline Nearne, another of the most successful girls, joined after she had been turned down by the army because she could not drive in the dark. Her sister Eileen joined after her.

Odette Churchill, a housewife with three children was discovered because she answered a radio appeal for snapshots of the French countryside. She replied to the wrong address. Shortly afterwards she had to make an enormous decision—should she leave her children and accept the risks and hardships of life with the French Resistance! After four months of harassing indecision she accepted, was captured in the field, survived and returned to be awarded the highest possible award for gallantry—the George Cross.

One little facet of Odette's story has always impressed me—

after returning from the German concentration camp and suffering torture, starvation and chaining-up by the Gestapo for two years, she was sent to see a doctor in London. She was still in her prison garb, distressed and bedraggled. 'I could yet hardly believe I was free. The doctor glanced at me and said, "I heard you have been a prisoner-of-war. How tiresome for a woman". Then I knew I was back in England and I could have hugged him,' she said. ('Tiresome'!)

The actual infiltration of the girls into the field was, in itself, a dangerous and risky operation. Most of them were dropped by parachute and met by reception committees which whisked them away swiftly to safe houses. Some of the landings were unusual. Christine Granville, the magnificent, casual heroine, dropped in a very high wind and hit the ground with such force that the butt of her revolver, in her hip pocket, was shattered though she was unhurt. Paddy O'Sullivan, a tomboy Irish wireless-operator, confessed to me that the one thing she was frightened of was cows—she had the terrifying (for her) experience of landing on the back of one.

One gentle young woman, Madeleine Damerment, through treachery, dropped to a 'reception committee' composed of the German security services. After the usual treatment and imprisonment she was shot through the back of the neck in a concentration camp. She died holding hands with another girl-agent, Elaine Plewman, who used to work for the Ministry of Information in London. She was also captured through treachery.

The first woman agent to be sent to France by the French section of SOE was a forty-seven-year-old grandmother, Yvonne Rudellat, a London hotel receptionist who first flew to Gibraltar in June 1942. The aircraft survived an attack by two German fighters; from there she sailed by small boat which was used for sardine fishing, called a felucca, to the shores of southern France. The boat survived a chase by an Italian corvette.

Four of the girls used the felucca method on their way to the field. Several were landed by aircraft on remote landing strips in the French countryside; two went by motor boat direct from England.

The aircraft generally used for landing agents was the Westland Lysander a single-engined high-wing aeroplane with a cruising speed of one hundred and sixty-four miles per hour. It could land and take off on a five-hundred-yard-long grass strip and could, besides the pilot, carry two passengers normally, three at a pinch and four in an emergency. The Lysanders frequently arrived back in England with leaves and branches of trees or high-tension electricity wires entangled on their wheels. Safely landed, the agent had at once to sink without trace into the anonymity of ordinary every-day life. She had to lead a double life carrying out her cover occupation as ordinarily as possible to avoid the notice of suspicious neighbours and the police and yet be available for Resistance duties. Lise de Baissac, one of the greatest of them, lived inconspicuously for months as a quiet widow interested in archaeology and Jacqueline Nearne, another great, re-adopted her peacetime occupation of a perfume saleswoman whilst carrying out her extremely valuable courier duties.

Baker Street spared neither trouble nor money to ensure that the girls were equipped as well as possible for their clandestine activities. Every attention was paid to their security before they left England. Scotland Yard detectives, amongst others, scrutinized the girls' clothing before they left. They searched, often with magnifying glasses, the turn-ups and the pockets, for even one shred of virginia tobacco or a tiny scrap of a London bus-ticket could 'give the show away' to German officials. SOE called on scientists and skilled craftsmen from some of Britain's most prestigious organizations and printing companies to turn out thousands of forged papers, passes, and official documents. The Germans were great believers in documents and they flooded France with official papers for railway journeys and admittance to factories, and with passes to men and women employed in war factories which allowed them to travel from their locality and break the curfew which was often enforced.

London produced forged copies of everything—some of

them so good as to be indistinguishable from the genuine article. Agents were well supplied with such papers before they left, or they were sent to them as required in the field. A Jewish refugee from Vienna was one of SOE's experts on clothing. His work earned him a captaincy in the British Army although he could hardly speak English. He ran a secret warehouse near Oxford Circus in London where a staff of Jewish tailors and seamstresses produced first-rate copies of genuine French suits, dresses, bodices and knickers. He used to go to synagogues all over London looking for refugees wearing the genuine articles which he bought or borrowed. He collected all the labels and name tags he found and inserted them in the agent's clothing. A Nottingham boot and shoe manufacturer produced French boots and shoes—most of which contained secret compartments in the heel or sole.

Secret codes were produced on micro-dots which could be hidden in any of the nooks and crannies of one's body. A matchstick was made in which in miniature the equivalent of nine sheets of writing on foolscap-size paper could be carried. The match was 'hidden' amongst ordinary matches in a box; toothpaste tubes, shoe laces and buttons were also used for hiding codes and messages. Codes were also printed on ties, scarves, handkerchiefs and underwear. Another way of remembering a code was through a stanza of verse which the agent learned by heart. The stanza had to be an original or obscure one in case the Germans knew it.

One example of a stanza from a 'respectable' agent is:

'Be near me when my light is low,
When the pulse beats fast
And the nerves prick and tingle
And all the wheels of being slow
Be near me when I fade away
To point the term of human strife
And on the low, dark verge of day
When twilight of external life
Be near me.'

The stanza that Rabelasian Nancy Wake used was:

'She stood right there
In the moonlight fair
And the moon shone through her nightie
It lit right on . . .'

At this stage the coding officer said he knew the concluding lines so unless somebody else knows them they will be lost for ever to posterity. It was soberly listed in SOE's code book.

3

THE TOP-SECRET TWO THOUSAND

In March 1945 it was revealed in a House of Commons debate that several young women had been parachuted, and in other ways infiltrated into enemy occupied France for active service against the German forces. It was sensational and the Press of the day splashed the news in startling headlines. It was particularly newsworthy because it had been such a well-kept secret. Later when more of the story was released the public learned that it was a secret that had been strictly and safely guarded—as closely as that of the confessional—by over two thousand women. This magnificent regiment of loyal and discreet women had been brought into being by a tough and experienced regular soldier who eventually became the head of all Britain's secret armies—Major-General Sir Colin Gubbins KCMG, DSC, MC, a Scot, who had taken part in guerrilla warfare during the 'troubles' in Ireland and India.

After the fall of France in 1940 when the Germans seemed poised for an immediate invasion of Britain, Sir Colin had been directed to organize British Resistance groups. He formed suicide squads of men who knew the countryside and volunteered to lie low whilst German forces passed through their areas and then to surface and attack them from the rear. He had hurriedly to prepare dumps of arms and explosives which were hidden in most unlikely places for the use of these squads and he needed trustworthy people to help. He knew the excellent work that the First Aid Nursing Yeomanry (The F.A.N.Y.s) had done under fire in the First World War so he phoned them. The Corps had remained in existence and trained without a break between the wars. At the beginning of the Second World War the majority of the serving members had been seconded to the motor transport companies of the ATS, but some members were working independently in various roles, notably with the Polish Army in Britain, and so Corps headquarters were kept going. It happened that a friend of his answered his call—Phyllis Bingham—and he told her what he wanted. A few days afterwards Phyllis Bingham and her colleague Peggy Minchin were seconded for duty with Sir Colin's organization. They had to sign the Official Secrets Act and, subsequently, spent an interesting and, at times, hair-raising period fusing and arming explosives for the use of suicide squads and also manning underground radio stations. The invasion scare passed but later when SOE was formed Sir Colin again remembered the F.A.N.Y.s. and called upon them to help not only in Britain but in several war zones all round the world.

The F.A.N.Y.s were a women's corps with a long and distinguished record. During the First World War they served in the front line at times—eighteen of them were awarded Military Medals for evacuating wounded men under fire and at the end of hostilities the corps had won ninety-five decorations for good and gallant service. It was a voluntary corps and its terms of service and discipline differ from those of the other women's services—later in the war F.A.N.Y.s in service units were paid service rates. Some girls who were obliged to register for war work were—if they were thought to be the right type—directed to report to F.A.N.Y.s Headquarters. Here they underwent searching interviews and their careers and backgrounds were probed. If all was well they were accepted to help in the vital work which the Corps was secretly carrying out.

A remarkably capable woman named Marian Gamwell was in charge of the F.A.N.Y.s recruited to help SOE. Not only had she to provide first-class recruits, she had also to ensure that the high tradition of the Corps was being maintained. As we have seen, the agents recruited for service in the field were also required to become members of the Corps—in their case because it provided a perfect cover for their clandestine activities. But even in their case Commandant Gamwell had the final decision about their suitability, and the right of veto. Some agents were serving members of the WAAF; they were seconded to the Corps during their service with SOE.

During the training of the women agents they were accompanied, shepherded, encouraged, watched over and catered for by F.A.N.Y.s. When the girls went into the field it was F.A.N.Y.s who manned the receiving sets in Britain waiting for their messages, sent them replies and coded and de-coded their messages. F.A.N.Y.s prepared and packed forged papers, passports and ration cards and filled the parachute containers with arms, explosives and supplies. As well as preparing the containers, F.A.N.Y.s packed the actual parachutes used in dropping the agents.

They manned over fifty schools and 'safe houses' in Britain doing the cooking, cleaning and washing, and catering. Frequently these 'safe houses' were occupied by groups of men who had finished their training and were waiting for the right time to be dropped in the war zones—France, Belgium, Holland, Norway, Poland. Often their waiting period was prolonged through bad weather or enemy action and to relieve their tension and monotony they were allowed to visit inns and taverns in the villages nearby. F.A.N.Y.s went with them to ensure security, stop them speaking to locals and to pay for their drinks because they usually had only foreign money with them. On one occasion this 'duty' placed a young and attractive F.A.N.Y. in a very embarrassing situation with her parents. She was seen in a pub near Windsor with a group of tough-looking men dressed in outlandish clothing—they usually wore the clothes they were to be dropped in—by a woman who knew her and her family. She saw the girl paying for the men's drinks and she was on the phone to the mother in double quick time next morning to warn her about the strange company her daughter was keeping. The worried parents protested to the girl the next time she came home on leave and warned her of the possible dire consequences of mixing with such people. The girl was not free to explain and she stumbled through a halting and unconvincing explanation which made the parents even more perturbed.

F.A.N.Y.s in uniform were a fairly common sight during the war in the streets of cities and in town and remote villages but nobody realized what they were doing. They were accepted as harmless and fairly useless girls who were enjoying a 'cushy' time. One mother who could not stand her daughter 'swanning around' in the neat uniform arranged an appointment for her in a local factory. 'You will be much more use there, and you will be helping the war effort,' the mother said. The girl was doing much more vital work—coding and de-coding. A sizeable number of F.A.N.Y.s were also working hard with services such as the British Red Cross Society and the Polish Army. Joachim Ronneberg, the Norwegian, and the six men he led to blow up the heavy-water plant in Norway which deprived the Germans of the atom bomb, were looked after by F.A.N.Y.s in a country house near Cambridge whilst they were waiting to be parachuted, he told me how good they were. One of his men, Captain Haukelid, in his book *Skis against the Atom* wrote—'It was a station for people who were going to Europe on secret errands and who had to wait for planes. The place was very closely guarded. A number of service women kept the house in order, cooked the meals, and gave the boys some social life. They belonged to the special section called F.A.N.Y.s. These girls did an uncommonly good job seeing that everything went as it should in the house and doing their best to prevent the delays from getting on our nerves. And when the Commandant allowed it they were always willing to come to Cambridge in the evening for a little party. The Commandant would allow a party if he was reasonably sure there would not be an operation next day. But if we asked the F.A.N.Y.s about our comrades who had gone out before us they became dumb and knew nothing.

'... the girls took good care of us in other ways too. They saw that we did not talk to strangers, that we did not catch cold, and that we came home in good order. We had a feeling of being fenced in and protected at every point from the dangers and difficulties of this world—that we might be used for one single purpose at home in Norway.

'... when one of our boys took a fancy to one of the prettiest F.A.N.Y.s he would spend the whole day scrubbing the kitchen table – and it needed it. We often washed and scrubbed for hours just to kill time. But however long we kept at it the F.A.N.Y.s were just as amiable—and unapproachable.'

F.A.N.Y. escorting-officers accompanied the women agents in their field training and weapon and parachute practice. One of these officers, Joan Windsor, actually completed thirty drops with her charges—to encourage and reassure them.

Another 'mother' accompanied her charge to the pistol-firing range. The agent was a young and completely inexperienced girl and loved making 'bangs' with the pistol but had no idea of how to direct them—she put a bullet clean through her 'mother's' skirt!

'Signals' was another vitally important branch staffed by F.A.N.Y.s. The wireless operator in the field had to keep strictly to scheduled times for transmitting and receiving. Her opposite number in Britain was a F.A.N.Y. who listened at the appointed time—it might, for instance, be between 7.30 and 8.00 p.m. But the Germans were also listening and they would immediately start 'jamming' the signals. In addition to this, natural atmospherics were often bad so the F.A.N.Y. had the greatest trouble in distinguishing the signals—but the F.A.N.Y. knew that if she asked for them to be repeated she would be giving the German 'D-Effers' more time to get a good 'fix' on the agent. The agent might also be suffering from extreme physical or mental strain which would affect the quality of her morse.

It was a difficult, tantalizing and unenviable job for the F.A.N.Y.—their average age was nineteen to twenty. Sometimes the agent would be late, sometimes, due to raids and arrests by the Germans, she could not transmit at all. The F.A.N.Y. in Britain sometimes had to wait fruitlessly with her head-phones on, hearing nothing but atmospheric noises for hours on end—it might be days, once there was nothing for six weeks. Still she waited.

The listening F.A.N.Y. also had to have her wits very much about her because she never knew when the message would include the special signal which meant that the sender was not sending a genuine message—she might be transmitting with the muzzle of a pistol at her head. It had been arranged during her training that if this ever happened she would transmit an agreed letter or phrase which would convey news of her predicament to London. The more experienced listening F.A.N.Y.s could tell by the sound of the morse who was transmitting, but the Germans knew this as well and on occasions tried to copy the style of the agent and send a false message. On one occasion a F.A.N.Y. in England was puzzled because the message ended with a long buzz—afterwards it was discovered that the agent had been shot through the head and had fallen across the key. Sometimes the messages received were far from warlike. One Christmas, instructions were asked for to cook a Christmas pudding which an agent had, somehow, come by. On another occasion the message was from a British officer who wanted to marry a wireless operator— a F.A.N.Y. He asked that Baker Street should put the banns up in an English church. This was done and the marriage and honeymoon took place under the noses of the unromantic Gestapo. A year later a message from the same Officer explained that the wireless operator was now about to have a baby and could the right kind of gear for such an event be forwarded. The F.A.N.Y.s at once took to their knitting needles, and Vera Atkins visited the right kind of shops, and a cylinder filled with napkins, socks and similar articles was dropped to a reception committee. Father, mother and son survived the war safely.

The uses of codes in wireless telegraphy was essential if the Germans were not to know what was going on and for the purposes of coding and de-coding the messages 120 F.A.N.Y.s were trained.

Mr Leo Marks, a brilliant and cheerful genius, was in charge of this department. In a radio programme which I wrote he was kind enough to give the following authentic reconstruction of an incident which happened on an occasion when he was sent a batch of twelve F.A.N.Y.s who had just finished their training. He purposely kept them waiting in a bare, chilly room until they were cross, tired and cold. He had also concealed a recording device in the room. When he eventually entered, he briefly excused himself and then pressed a switch which played the recording of everything which had been said in the room—parts of it quite embarrassing. When the recording was finished he told the girls—

'You've been kept waiting in a cold room to make you tired and irritable, because when you're tired and irritable you grow careless. And when you're careless, you're talkative. I promise you that before you've been with us long, you'll be limp—but next time you feel like talking, remember that button on the wall. The Germans have recorders too, where you'd least expect them to be placed. Each one of you has a crowd of admirers you've never met. Don't get excited—they're Gestapo admirers.

'They work in the Gestapo cipher section, trying to break our agents' codes. But they can't break them, and you girls are their only chance. They welcome you today, because they hope you're green enough to want to boast. You'll have plenty to boast about. You're important people. You're going to be told about things you shouldn't know—but we can't help ourselves, we've got to trust you.

'Every department has its secrets—but you in codes will read all the secrets of all the departments. If you talk about any of them, a man will die. It's as simple as that. Now, I'm never going to mention security to you again.

'You think you're tired, don't you? Then imagine how tired an agent feels who's had no sleep for three nights and has to code a message. The Germans are all around her. She has no electric light, no table, no supervisor to check her work. All she has is a vital message that must reach England. Hasn't that girl a right to make a mistake in her coding? And if she makes a mistake, must she be penalized for it? Must she come on the air and repeat her message, while every moment German direction-finding cars are closing in on her, getting her bearings?

'She must—if we can't decode it. It is our privilege to see that no agent has to risk arrest because we in the coding department can't find the mistake. Last week, the coders at the home station tried thirty seven thousand attempts to break a message—and succeeded on the thirty-seven thousand and second . . . twelve minutes before an agent was due to come on the air and repeat it.

'Now today, I've got to ask your help. We're up against the toughest problem this department has ever had. There is an agent in Belgium surrounded by the Boche. He is completely cut-off. He has sent a message telling us where he can be picked up. A Lysander aircraft is standing by. Everything is ready to rescue him—but we cannot decode his message. So far, we have tried over forty thousand attempts—and it will not budge. At eight o'clock this evening he is due to come on the air and repeat it. If he does—those cars will close in. We will lose that man.

'Now . . . on your behalf, I see every agent who goes into the field and I make them a promise. I tell them—on your behalf—that if they make a mistake there are a hundred and twenty girls in England who will break their message for them. A hundred and twenty girls who will know no rest until their mistake is discovered and put right. We have got to break this message before eight o'clock tonight. You are going down as reinforcements. You will be told what to do by your colleagues. You will find that they are tired, tense, sulky—and the salt of the earth. None of them is quite sane—but don't worry, you'll soon be like them. Sleep in the train going down—sleep in the coach that waits at the station—sleep when you shake hands with your Commanding Officer—but don't sleep in the code room.

'Any one of you may hit upon the key that breaks this message. Our agent's life is going to be saved. He knows it is. He trusts you. Don't grow old too quickly and don't stay young too long. Good luck—good coding, and remember . . . you're all that agent's got . . .' The girls joined the others already working on that garbled message and after 56,000 permutations the correct version emerged. There was then eight minutes to spare, the Lysander took off and the agent was brought safely back to England.

After the war Sir Colin Gubbins wrote to Commandant Gamwell: 'I am left tongue-tied when I try to tell you what the F.A.N.Y.s have meant to the organization and to me. I say to me because I took the original decision and had the idea to use them to the utmost, and I am personally sufficiently human to be glad to find my judgement proved right. But to the Organization they were everything, as you well know, and without them we just could not have done it. In every theatre they have become a household word for efficiency, guts, cheerfulness, persistence, tenacity and comradeship in difficulty and I am proud to have been the means of their proving their great qualities, they have been magnificent, and invaluable. I know that what they have themselves learnt will be of inestimable and permanent value to their country'.

4

VIRGINIA, THE GRANDMOTHER, AND PADDY

The first and one of the greatest and most remarkable of the 'British' girls who went to France to work for Special Operations Executive was an American girl—'Marie of Lyons'. She, and Cuthbert, entered France from Spain in August 1941. She was Virginia Hall—her field name was Mary—and Cuthbert was her wooden leg. She settled down in the city of Lyons as an accredited correspondent of the New York Post—America was not yet in the war so she passed as a neutral journalist—but she could not have had much time for journalism because she threw herself enthusiastically into the business of organizing the Resistance. She became a tireless and invaluable 'godmother' to all the other men and women agents and their assistants who entered or passed through her area. She kept up a constant flow of information to London through her wireless operators and answered all London's queries about conditions, agents and suspected traitors. She was deeply involved in the escape networks ushering escaped service men from all the services to Spain and Switzerland; she found dropping zones for supplies and landing-strips for aircraft; arranged to supply food to men and women in the jails, patched up internal strife; arranged escapes from prisons; stored arms, money and wireless sets, which she distributed as required, and acted as a recruiting agency for SOE and the Resistance forces—in fact, she ran a busy kind of de-centralized H.Q.

Virginia's never-ending activity over such a wide range of interests had, of course, to be as secret as possible. Inevitably, however, loose talkers and traitors were a constant threat to her organization and to the safety of its members. And, inevitably also, the Gestapo heard and went hot-foot on her trail. They arrived in Lyons in November 1942 and their leader was heard to say—'I'd give anything to lay my hands on that Canadian bitch'. His knowledge of North American nationalities was limited. He missed her!

'Marie of Lyons' and Cuthbert had bolted with speed and discretion and safely completed a hazardous and difficult crossing of the Pyrenees mountains into Spain. But she was arrested on arrival and sent to a Spanish prison. SOE pulled strings and she was released through diplomatic intervention, and returned to England. She had completed fifteen invaluable months in the field. The comparative peace of England did not suit her and she was soon badgering SOE to be returned to the war-zone as a courier. Influenced no doubt by Cuthbert, the organization would not agree; they also knew that the Germans now knew her identity and were aware of all her activities. But she was persistent. She learned the Morse code privately and how to maintain and operate a wireless set—she was accepted back and returned to France in March 1944. Her task this time was to visit the scattered groups of Maquis, to help organize and train them, stir up their aggressive spirit and get them busy on sabotage. She survived the war safely.

Elizabeth Reynolds was twenty-seven years old when the Hudson aircraft she was in shuddered to a halt and left her a bit shaken but otherwise unharmed on French soil. During the landing one of its wings had struck the belfry of a church, but the pilot managed to control it, land safely and fly immediately back to England.

She was tall, ginger-haired, dignified. Educated at a girls' public school in the south of England she was the most English-looking girl of all who became secret agents, so much so that it became necessary to recall her—she too was an American. She was sent to the field because during training she had proved herself eminently capable; in the field she carried out her duties conscientiously, efficiently and without the slightest concern about her own safety. In training she was the best of her group, she took unarmed combat in her magnificent stride, sabotage, shooting and detonating explosives came easily to her, rock-climbing, mountaineering and forced marches over the difficult Scottish countryside delighted her, she was good at sports and an excellent skier. She had been living with her mother in France when it was occupied by the Germans. She decided to go to England, made her way to southern France and tackled the redoubtable Pyrenees, 'It was the most awful experience of my life,' she said afterwards.

She was everything one expected an English 'county' girl to look like—an aristocratic nose, calm—almost insolent stare—drank well, wore tweeds and was imperturbable. 'SOE were mad to send her to France as she stuck out like a sore thumb,' wrote her Commanding Officer, Colonel Richard Heslop, one of the legendary heroes of the Resistance.

He wrote this in his great book *Xavier*, which was his code name in the field. He wrote also of his great admiration for Elizabeth: 'She did a fine job, for she had guts and imagination'. One great asset she had as a courier was an excellent memory, she could memorize a message and repeat it verbatim so that she had no need to carry scraps of paper nor, as some couriers did, to write the messages on obscure parts of their body.

Just before D-day (6th June 1944) Colonel Heslop had the unpleasant task of telling Elizabeth that she had been recalled to England. The only reason was that she looked so English and whilst the Colonel and the other members of the Resistance were concerned about her own safety they also had to take into consideration that this might endanger the safety of the whole group. She was very upset and pleaded to be allowed to stay, but the Colonel was obliged to be adamant. She left, but was foolhardy enough to travel to Paris where her mother was living. She adored her mother who had been imprisoned by the Germans but released on account of her bad health, but they kept her under close supervision. Elizabeth went to the house and was arrested. She was not badly treated because the Gestapo could not shake her cover story and never discovered her connection with SOE. She was liberated when the Allies overran Paris.

George Millar, journalist and author who distinguished himself with the Resistance, also mentions Elizabeth with affection and admiration in his book *Horned Pigeon*. He recalled that when he first met her on a remote farm in France, she was dressed in 'a handsome costume of brown tweed, extremely well cut with a divided skirt'. In her rucksack, slung on her shoulder, was a magnificent dressing case with gold fittings and containing gold-backed brushes and combs—it was worth, then, about a million and a half French francs.

The first woman to be clandestinely infiltrated to France was a grandmother. Cheerful, intelligent and active, Yvonne Rudellat was nearly fifty when she disembarked from a little fishing boat on the southern coast of France. She was very young when she married an Italian antique dealer who lived in London, and brought up two daughters. Before the war she managed a decorating business in west London and when that closed down became the manageress of a small hotel in the same area. One of the guests, impressed by the calm efficiency of Yvonne, was connected with SOE, and through him she was interviewed, accepted for training, and finally approved for service in the field. The 'reception committee' service in France was then in its infancy, so she was flown to Gibraltar to take a felucca to France. It was quite an eventful journey. Her aircraft was attacked by two German fighters who shot away one of the engines and it limped to Gibraltar at about fifty feet above the waters of the Mediterranean. Sailing to France, her boat was seen and chased by an Italian patrol boat, but it escaped and she landed safely in the darkness.

She was most unfortunate with her first C.O. who turned out to be one of the failures of the organization. He actually reported to London that she had gone over to the Germans which caused amazement in Baker Street. It was true that she was a very new agent but such a possibility was quite at variance with her character so they sent an officer out to find out what was happening. He very quickly vindicated Yvonne who then began an 'explosive' career in the field which led to consternation and death in the ranks of the occupying Germans.

Her new C.O. a Frenchman named Culuoli, and Yvonne

operated in a wild, wooded hunting region south of Paris through which several important roads and railways passed. They and their groups became a scourge to the Germans and their communications. When she was not arranging landing-strips and dropping zones for containers she was actively engaged in aggressive sabotage—blowing up factories, demolishing electricity pylons, wrecking railway sheds, derailing troop trains and planting time-bombs on goods trains.

It became the most dangerous area in France for the Germans and they reacted by swamping it with troops and tanks—trying ruthlessly to crush the resistance and capture the woman leader. At length they did. There are conflicting reports of the moment of capture—she was seriously wounded before they laid their hands on her and she may well have been firing her revolver at them until she became unconscious, but it is not possible to confirm all the details. However, it is known that she and Culuoli were ordered to drive two Canadian wireless operators to Paris at a time when the German counter activity in the area was at its height. On the way the car ran into a heavy German road block. They were stopped and forced to drive to the headquarters of the SS troops for questioning. Culuoli and Yvonne produced their papers which satisfied the Germans and they were allowed to leave the building and sit in the car to wait until the Germans were finished with the other two. Suddenly a German officer ran from the building and ordered them to get out of the car. Culuoli guessed that the game was up—he started up, pushed hard on the accelerator and shot away as fast as he could. SS troops piled into three powerful cars and gave chase—when they came within range the Germans opened fire and two bullets hit Yvonne who slumped across her C.O. He went on but bullets shattered his windscreen so that he could not see properly and he ran into a brick wall and was knocked unconscious. The Germans pulled them both from the wrecked car and he recovered consciousness to find them kicking him, he kicked back so they shot him through the knee.

Yvonne spent many weeks in hospital and was operated on several times. When she became convalescent the doctors and nurses at the hospital conceived an escape plot for her, but the day before it was to be implemented the Germans moved her to Paris for interrogation. Later she was sent to the notorious concentration camp at Belsen. Tragically, when this dreadful place was overrun by British troops on 15 April 1945 Yvonne was still just alive. Ravaged by starvation, typhus and dysentry she died unknown and undiscovered a day or two later. She was buried, one of the twenty thousand others, in one of the mass graves.

Major Phillipe de Vomecourt was one of the acknowledged heroes of the Resistance. After three years reliable work in the field he was captured but managed to escape, made his way across the Pyrenees and arrived at Baker Street in London. He spent his time in England preparing for his return to France and just before he left, in April 1944, was given a choice of four assistants to take with him. He chose a little dark-haired ex-WAAF who was parachuted to his sector in France on 9th April 1944 with her wireless set. Phillipe, who could not parachute because of an old injury, followed by Lysander aircraft a few days later.

Little Muriel Byck was risking even more than the others in going into the field because she was a Jewess who stuck to her faith until she died. Afterwards Phillipe recalled, 'She looked so young but I had seen enough in France to know that courage knew no barrier of age'. She was plunged straightaway into one of the most active and successful sectors of the Resistance. Tirelessly and efficiently she carried out her duties—she religiously maintained her 'skeds', as they were called, that is the scheduled hours for listening to and sending messages to London Headquarters. And between 'skeds' she acted as a courier taking messages to and from members of the group through the German-patrolled roads and countryside. She used a shed behind a garage as her listening post and frequently watched German troops bringing their vehicles to the garage for repairs.

She became heavily involved when her C.O. planned a combined operation with London in which Allied bombers would attack a huge arms dump to coincide with attacks by the

Resistance. The dumps, which covered over fifty acres, supplied shells and explosives to the Germans guarding the French coast against invasion, and bombs to the German airforce.

Muriel handled all the radio traffic for the operation and, like Yvonne Baseden at Dole, sat glued to her set as the British and American bombers approached their target. First came the Pathfinders dropping their flares to mark the target, then the main force came in dropping hundreds of tons of high explosive bombs which wrecked the dump causing enormous detonations and great fires which illuminated the devastated area. And as the German troops bolted from the target area they were harassed and exterminated by the land-mines, booby traps and attacks of the Resistance fighters, organized by Phillipe.

But Muriel was sickening at the time and the terrific airraid, explosions and havoc did not help. She moved to a blacksmith's house where she became very ill and a Resistance doctor diagnosed meningitis and said that hospital treatment was essential. It was dangerous at any time then for members of the resistance to be treated in hospitals, which were closely watched and regularly inspected by the Germans. It was many times more dangerous in that area after the successful attack on the dump because the German were infuriated and were taking savage retaliations. However, Phillipe insisted and drove Muriel to a hospital run by nuns and told them that he was her uncle. Operations were performed but Muriel grew worse and died on 23rd May in the arms of her 'Uncle'.

She was buried under a false name watched by the Gestapo and Phillipe, who insisted on being present, had to escape by scaling the cemetery wall. Her grave was carefully tended by the French country people during the war; afterwards the body was brought to England and re-buried under her right name. She had been active in the field for little more than a month but during that time had risked everything, worked ceaselessly and earned the affection, admiration and respect of all who knew her.

Denise Bloch was also a Jewess. She was executed by shooting through the back of the neck at Ravensbruck concentration camp in March. Shot with her were Violette Szabo, the little ex-Woolworth's shop assistant from Brixton, London, posthumously awarded the George Cross and Lilian Rolfe, another agent who used to live in Woking near London. Denise had worked with the resistance in France before escaping to England and joining SOE. She became a wireless operator and was sent to France by Lysander on 3rd March 1944 to join a circuit near Paris run by Robert Benois, one time famous motor racing driver. He was a formidable Resistance fighter who was also captured eventually and hanged at Buchenwald concentration camp. Before his capture he had led the Germans a merry dance and had several thrilling escapes. Once, seated between two German soldiers in an open car in which he was being driven to prison, he suddenly pushed one of them out and jumped after him. Both of them rolled on the roadway, Robert scrambled to his feet and bolted. He was a member of a wealthy family who owned a château near Paris. He was finally captured at one of these when he went to see his mother who had become very ill, Denise was captured the following day in another Benois château and lodged in the notorious Fresnes prison where the Germans were holding 1,600 other patriots.

Denise had joined SOE under the name of Danielle Williams and was known in the field as Ambroise. The official orders handed to her C.O. Robert Benois before he left England contains the following paragraph which explains the position of the agents who worked as wireless operators—'You will be accompanied to the field by Ambroise, who is to act as your W/T operator. She will be under your command, but it must be understood that she is the ultimate judge in all questions regarding the technicalities of W/T and W/T security. She will encode the messages herself. They should be as short and clear as possible, since it is of the utmost importance that her time on the air should be reduced to the minimum'.

Early in 1944 the demand for wireless operators became

urgent and every effort was made to hasten their training. Indeed, some of them had a shortened training and when the brothers P. E. and E. P. Mayer were dropped into central France to take over a circuit it was a hastily trained young Irishwoman who was dropped to them with her wireless transmitting set a fortnight later. She was Maureen O'Sullivan, daughter of the editor of an Irish national newspaper called *The Freeman's Journal.* She had been brought up in French convents, was bi-lingual, very attractive and quite fearless. That is, she told me, fearless of anything except cows—they terrified her. So, although she had many narrow escapes in France, her worst experience, she says, was the moment she landed. She had dropped into a herd of cows and landed on the back of one! The 'reception committee' rescued her and lodged her in a safe house near a barracks occupied by German soldiers—she was given a bicycle, and when she confessed that she could not ride it, was ordered to master it. So the following day she took it onto the roadway and began to practise—much to the amusement of a group of German soldiers. 'Paddy'—everybody called her that—became annoyed and abused them saying that if they were gentlemen they would help her, which they did. With their aid she became proficient and was then sent off to a remote farm to begin her work.

On another occasion she had a far more dangerous brush with Germans, when only her charm and quick wit saved her from capture and all that that would have entailed. She had to pick up a wireless set to take to the farm and the only transport available was her bicycle. She wrapped it up, tied it on the carrier and set off through what was usually a safe and unpatrolled road. That day, however, the Germans had set up a surprise road-block and she was obliged to dismount and produce her papers. She kept her head and began to smile and flirt with them—they became quite human and forgot all about the parcel on her carrier, she made an appointment to meet them later that evening and they cheerfully waved her on with good wishes and *aufwiedersehens*—but they were, of course, disappointed.

She maintained a regular and busy contact with London headquarters from the remote farmhouse. One afternoon she was transmitting to London from the kitchen when the woman of the house called out in alarm that a lorry load of Germans had turned into the track leading to the house and were driving up. The old grandmother was sitting in her usual chair in the kitchen and there was a pot of meat boiling over the open fire. Swiftly the old lady stood up and the wireless set was placed on the chair, she sat on it and spread out her voluminous skirts to conceal it. Paddy, dressed like a country girl, sat by the simmering pot stirring it and holding the messages she had been transmitting in her hands. Soldiers came into the kitchen so Paddy dropped her messages into the stew and continued her stirring, but they only wanted to know if there were any eggs they could buy. The old lady abused them, Paddy went on silently stirring, the housewife collected some eggs and handed them over. Then the soldiers left.

Paddy continued her work and was safe and well when allied troops overran the area later in the year.

5

THE WILD COLONIAL GIRL

Nancy Wake was wearing high-heeled shoes, had a revolver in each pocket of her trousers and was carrying a million francs when she arrived by parachute—safely on a hedge—in France at one o'clock in the morning of 29th February 1944. Nancy was not a wireless operator, nor a courier; she was sent to join, help organize, pay and help arm and report on one of the toughest groups of Maquis in the wildest mountain region of central France—and magnificently did the 'wild colonial girl' carry out her mission.

She was then twenty-six years old, attractive, handsomely built, utterly fearless, supremely self-confident and deeply dedicated to the task of frustrating and spreading havoc amongst the German forces of whom she had already had bitter and unforgettable experience. Nancy was an Australian who had been an attendant in a mental hospital before becoming a journalist in Sydney. In 1935 she decided to see the world, paying her way as a freelance journalist. In 1939, when she was twenty-four, she met and married a splendid Frenchman, named Henri Fiocca, at Marseilles. He was a wealthy industrialist and Nancy lived in great happiness and luxury until the Germans attacked France. She persuaded her husband to fit out one of his motor vans as an ambulance and she drove right through France as near as possible to the fighting lines where she gave what help she could to the wounded. When the Germans broke through and the roads were thick with fleeing evacuees she witnessed all the horrors of total war—the bombing and machine-gunning of men, women and children, the merciless slaughter, the panic, the terror. France capitulated and she returned to Marseilles.

One evening she was having a drink in a bar at the Hôtel du Louvre when she noticed a youngish man reading an English book. She wondered whether he was a member of the Gestapo or an Englishman and when her husband joined her she asked him to find out. Henri got into conversation with the man and came back to tell her that he was one of two hundred British officers who had been captured and were lodged in a nearby prison. This one had been granted parole and had come to the hotel for a drink. Henri and Nancy subsequently entertained all these officers—in relays—to receptions and dinners at their home. One of these was a Captain Garrow who was a member of SOE and who later escaped from the prison and set up an escape route for British servicemen across the Pyrenees to neutral Spain, from where they were transported back to Britain. This escape route later became the very famous 'Pat O'Leary escape line' called after the organizer, a Belgian who adopted the very Irish pseudonym.

Nancy started by acting as courier to Captain Garrow and when he left she became Pat O'Leary's 'right-hand man'. She worked for two and a half years on this escape route which was responsible for shepherding over one thousand people back to Britain. The Gestapo learned of her activities but did not discover her identity—but she had many narrow escapes. Once she was captured and lodged in a Police station many miles from Marseilles—she refused to say who she was and why she was there. O'Leary arrived and, by a gigantic bluff, persuaded the police to release her—he told them that she was his mistress and that she would not talk because she did not want to betray his unfaithfulness! But O'Leary was betrayed and captured and the Gestapo came hot on the trail of Nancy so that she had to run for it. After she left, Henri too was betrayed—they tortured him savagely but could not make him talk so they shot him. Now Nancy had to face the difficult crossing of the Pyrenees in rigorous winter conditions. With a small party and two guides she set out to walk, climb and claw her way over the snow covered peaks. It took seventy-four hours with ten minutes rest every two hours, part of the time they had to battle with fierce blizzard conditions. But they made it and Nancy was sponsored by the British authorities in Spain, sent to Gibraltar and from there to Britain by ship, in June 1943.

Captain Garrow was then working with SOE in London and through him she volunteered and was accepted for training by SOE. Nancy was not the most amenable of pupils and did not hide her dislike for the physical effort demanded. Climbing high walls, crossing rivers on ropes, running through difficult country, and above all getting up at dawn for PT was not her idea of life. At one training unit she was the only woman and when they woke her for PT in the cold darkness of dawn she said she was not feeling well. Allowing for her femininity they left her, but when the same excuse continued for several days they became a little doubtful and eventually worried so one morning they sent a doctor to examine her—she jumped quickly out of bed and on to the barrack square, like a shot. She did not like jumping from the captive balloon in the parachute training either, and she agreed to do the last jump only because each of the men in the party agreed to buy her a double whisky. Nancy had learned a lot in Marseilles including a wide vocabulary from the fish-markets and an enormous capacity for alcohol.

When I met her in London after the war she told me about the incident of the bottle of George IV Scotch whisky, Henri and the traitor. She was saving up this bottle of whisky—which was then very rare in war-ravaged France—for Henri's birthday and she hid it in the flat. At that time a man of whom she was highly suspicious used to come to the flat listening and drinking anything that was available. One evening Nancy returned to find Henri and this man very merry and on the table was the empty bottle of George IV—Nancy was astonished and immediately indignant—she asked Henri where he had found the whisky. He had not known about it, he said, the other man had found it somewhere in the flat. Nancy was furious and not so much about the whisky but about the impertinence of the fellow in searching their personal hiding places—she told him what she thought of him and booted him unceremoniously down the stairs. (I felt so sorry about that bottle of whisky that I told a member of the distilling company about the incident—he immediately sent me another bottle to give to Nancy. I was in bed with influenza when it arrived, so I phoned Nancy and told her. She said to bring it straight along and we would deal with it together, but I explained about the 'flu. 'Then drink it, you silly blighter,' she said 'and get better'. So I did and as I have not seen her since, I still owe her a bottle of George IV!)

One of the instructors she met during training was Captain Denis Rake, MC, Legion of Honour, who had already completed one mission in France and was to see a lot more action there with Nancy. He was an actor who came from a well-known theatrical family—they were in Brussels when he was born. In the First World War Denis' father was caught helping Nurse Cavell's escape organization and was executed by the Germans at St Giles Prison like her. Denis became a music hall singer and appeared in many musicals in London including *No, No, Nanette* with Binnie Hale, and with Ivor Novello at Drury Lane Theatre.

Captain John Farmer, an arms instructor, dropped with Nancy—they were told that Maurice Southgate, whom they expected to meet, had been arrested. After a few days in a safe house they travelled to and met the Maquis and their chief. They met a really tough bunch of desperadoes living rough in the mountain fastness, disorganized and lacking arms and concerted purpose. The Maquis were not a whit impressed by the arrival from London of a mission consisting of one officer and a woman! The Maquis knew, however, that she had a lot of money with her and the detailed plans for their target on D-day. To make matters worse she had no wireless operator so, they argued amongst themselves, what on earth good were the newcomers. They decided that the best thing to do was to kill Captain Farmer, seduce Nancy, take her money and plans and then kill her.

They underestimated Nancy and her companion. They overheard the plot and were not, obviously, enamoured with it. Nancy confronted the leader and in no uncertain language told him what she thought of him and his gang, adding that it would have to be a far better man than he had available to seduce her, that there was a wireless operator on the way and that she was their only chance of securing arms and ammunition. She convinced him, and then deeply impressed him by her conduct when she insisted on joining a raid they had planned on a bootstore in a town with a large German garrison.

A few days afterwards Denis Rake, her ex-instructor arrived. He was a thoroughly skilled wireless operator as well as a most amusing companion. Soon he was tapping out the messages that Nancy prepared—lists of supplies, guns, grenades, explosives and more money. Now the position of the three Britishers was completely transformed—they became now the vital and valuable link with a headquarters able and willing to supply everything the Maquis needed.

Whilst Denis sent his messages and kept his schedules with London, Nancy chose dropping zones and arranged reception committees, and John Farmer taught the men how to use the new weapons and plastic explosives. More and more recruits joined the Maquis and it eventually became a formidable force of seven thousand well-disciplined men. Night after night bombers from Britain zoomed over the area dropping hundreds of containers full of supplies and war materials.

She now had to assume the duties of paymaster and quartermaster. Money was dropped to her and she had to be on the zone to receive it—she paid out as much as 15,000,000 francs a month (then about £85,000) to the men and allowances and pensions to dependents.

Just before D-day she handed out the list of targets which were to be attacked and on the night preceding the landing the Maquis played havoc with the German communications and wrecked electrical installations and other targets over a wide area. The destruction the Maquis caused spurred the Germans to savage reprisals—the area became reminiscent of the wild west of America when roving bands of Indians used to raid lonely farmhouses. Nancy passed many burnt-out houses with mutilated corpses littering the ground and bodies hanging from trees.

The Germans determined to put a stop to the Maquis and

threw a force of twenty-two thousand troops supported by artillery, armoured cars, bombers and spotting aircraft, against them. A great battle ensued against the seven thousand now well-armed and well dug-in patriots defending the heights and plateaus. Nancy was in the thick of the battle driving a van with more ammunition, mortar bombs and grenades to where-ever they were needed. She was spotted driving across an open road by two German fighters which swooped on her, raking the road and the back of the van with machine-gun fire. One of them swooped again and she leaped from the van a moment before it was peppered with bullets and blown up in flames.

When the night came the Maquis, guerrilla-fashion, retired higher into the mountains leaving a hundred of their dead behind and one thousand five hundred dead Germans.

But a very serious loss that the Maquis sustained was the loss of all Denis Rake's wireless codes. He had to destroy them when he was in danger of capture and without them could not contact London and without that contact the whole Maquis force would soon become just a demoralized rabble without arms, ammunition or supplies. It became of vital and immediate importance that somehow a message should be passed to SOE informing them of the loss and requesting new codes—but there was nobody anywhere near who could do this. This circumstance led to Nancy's historic and heroic bicycle ride and trek through difficult mountain terrain abounding with enemy troops who were then very angry and alert—a ride of three hundred miles in seventy-two hours. She eventually and after several narrow escapes found a Free French operator who sent the message to London via his own headquarters in North Africa. She passed through several villages garrisoned by Germans and past guarded road-blocks. Once she had to leave her bicycle hidden in bracken and sit in a farmer's cart pretending to be his dumb daughter—daubing her face and straggling her hair to play the part. They were stopped and searched a dozen times but the 'dumb daughter' was ignored. She arrived safely back at the Maquis stronghold in a most distressed condition and it took three days before she was fit again.

The parachuting resumed immediately and the precious containers rained down again on the dropping zones. The Germans continued to launch sporadic attacks on the Maquis and Nancy was involved in several skirmishes. Once in action against seven thousand Germans—for which she was awarded the American Medal of Freedom with Bronze Palm—she stood her ground and advanced when others fled. She was with two American officers armed with bazookas, the three of them destroyed a number of armoured cars and several machine-gun posts. And at night she was back on the dropping zones checking the reception committees and the containers—sometimes there was a container addressed to her filled with gifts of face cream, powder, lip-sticks, sweets and good wishes from her friends at headquarters.

There was a Gestapo headquarters in the nearby town of Montlucon which was also strongly garrisoned by German troops. It was decided to attack the headquarters and Nancy with fourteen companions in four cars drove straight into the town and pulled up outside the building at 12.25 one afternoon. She jumped from the car, ran up the stairs of the building, threw open a door and hurled a hand grenade, as she ran down the stairs it exploded. Her companions were doing the same thing all over the house—they escaped leaving a shattered headquarters and thirty-eight dead members of the force.

On another occasion it was planned to attack and demolish a factory which was manufacturing vital parts for the Germans. The factory was guarded by four pairs of German sentries at each of the four gates—Nancy was in charge of one party detailed to put two of the guards out of commission. Dashing from cover she approached one of the sentries determined to knock him out—but he turned quickly shifting his rifle and opening his mouth to shout a warning. Nancy leapt and struck him a karate-like blow she had been taught in the SOE training school. She was subsequently not a little distressed to discover how effective it was—the sentry was dead before he touched the ground. All the sentries were accounted for and the factory successfully blown to bits.

The Germans were now being repeatedly and successfully

harassed and becoming ragged—the rout was beginning. They were more dangerous than ever, however, because they were frightened of the retribution that the Resistance forces and the population might take for the ruthless reign of terror which they had previously maintained. There were short bitter actions being fought constantly all over the area.

Nancy who had been living most of the time in a cramped caravan in the mountains began to think of improving her quarters and set her heart upon a huge château in its own grounds, six miles from Montlucon. It had been empty for years, but could easily be put into habitable condition—she set engineers and electricians about making it ready and they moved in. They were barely in when the Germans decided to leave Montlucon and Nancy was told that there was a huge German convoy approaching the mansion—she ordered everybody inside and closed all the windows and doors. The convoy ignored the empty-looking château and trundled past heading towards the Fatherland. Allied aircraft were still dropping containers every night so she had the inspired idea of fitting floodlights about the park area in front of the château and using it as the dropping zone. The Reception Committee could now relax comfortably in bed until the drop was over and then emerge on their front lawn to collect the containers!

As the Germans withdrew a great feeling of relief and jubilation prevailed and there were numerous parties and celebrations at which the British and American agents were toasted and expected to reciprocate, especially by singing their national anthems. Nancy and her British friends knew enough of 'God Save the King' to oblige, but her two American companions were in a quandary because although they knew the air of 'The Star Spangled Banner' they knew none of the words. However, they improvized very successfully by substituting the words of a rhyme which went:

Uncle George and Auntie Mabel
Fainted at the breakfast table
Wasn't that sufficient warning not to do it in the morning?
But Ovaltine has put them right

Now they do it morn and night
Uncle George is hoping soon
To do it in the afternoon.

They sang this to the air of 'Hark! The Herald Angels Sing' and explained that it was a new American Anthem in honour of the Entente Cordiale. It was very well received by the French. Conscious of the great honour of a new anthem, the company stood rigidly to attention when it was sung by the Americans who were usually joined enthusiastically by their British colleagues and it earned long and sincere ovations.

On her twenty-seventh birthday the Maquis paid Nancy a tremendous compliment. Hundreds of them turned up at the Château and Nancy stood clutching a huge bunch of flowers they had given her, with her officers, as they marched past giving her the Maquis salute.

The news arrived that the Germans were to evacuate Vichy, the town that gave its name to the French traitor-Government, and Nancy hurried there to lead her men in the victory parade.

After the war Nancy worked in London for a time with the Air Ministry before re-marrying and returning to live in Australia. The British Government awarded Nancy the George Medal. The following was the citation:

Ensign Nancy Grace Augusta Wake, FANY.
George Medal citation.

This officer was parachuted into France on the 1st March 1944 as assistant to an organizer who was taking over the direction of an important circuit in central France. The day after her arrival she and her chief found themselves stranded and without directions, through the arrest of their contact, but ultimately reached their rendezvous by their own initiative.

Ensign Wake worked for several months helping to train and recruit Maquis groups. She took part in several engagements with the enemy, and showed the utmost bravery under fire. During a German attack, due to the arrival by parachute of two young American officers to help in the Maquis, Ensign Wake personally took command of a section of ten men whose leader was demoralized. She led them to within point-blank range of the enemy, directed their fire, rescued the two American officers and withdrew in good order. She showed exceptional courage and coolness in the face of enemy fire.

When the Maquis group with which she was working was broken up by large-scale German attacks, and W/T contact was lost, Ensign Wake went alone to find a wireless operator through whom she could contact London. She covered some 200 kilometres on foot and by remarkable steadfastness and perseverance succeeded in getting a message through to London giving the particulars of a ground where a new W/T plan and further stores could be dropped. It was largely due to these efforts that the circuit was able to start work again.

Ensign Wake's organizing ability, endurance, courage and complete disregard for her own safety earned her the respect and admiration of all with whom she came in contact. The Maquis troop, most of them rough and difficult to handle, accepted orders from her, and treated her as one of their own male officers. Ensign Wake contributed in a large degree to the success of the groups with whom she worked, and it is strongly recommended that she be awarded the George Medal.

The Americans awarded her the Medal of Freedom with Bronze Palm, one of the few foreigners ever to receive it. The following was the citation:

Citation for the Medal of Freedom with Bronze Palm.

Ensign Nancy Wake, British National, FANY, for exceptionally meritorious achievement which aided the United States in the prosecution of the war against the enemy in continental Europe, from March 1944 to October 1944. After having been parachuted into the Allied Department of France for the purpose of co-ordinating Resistance activities, she immediately assumed her duties as second-in-command to the organizer of the circuit. Despite numerous difficulties and personal danger she, through her remarkable courage, initiative and coolness succeeded in accomplishing her objective. Her daring courage in the course of an enemy engagement safeguarded the lives of two American officers under her command. Her inspiring leadership, bravery, and exemplary devotion to duty contributed materially to the success of the war effort and merit the praise and recognition of the United States.

GO 3. Hq USFET, 9th January 1947.

The French Government awarded her the coveted Resistance Medal, two Croix de Guerre with Palm and a third Croix de Guerre with Star.

6

JACQUELINE AND PEARL

Mr Nearne, an Englishman, and his wife of Spanish origin had a family of two daughters, Jacqueline born in Brighton on 27th May 1916, Eileen born in London in 1921, and two sons, Francis born in 1914 and Frederick in 1920. Three of the Nearne children, Jacqueline, Eileen and Francis distinguished themselves magnificently in one of Britain's most hazardous services—SOE. They all saw service in the field and Eileen survived a German capture and concentration camps without ever revealing a word about her companions or, indeed, that she was an English-born secret agent working for the French Resistance. Surely, the Nearnes hold an unique, honourable family record.

In 1923 when Jacqueline was seven the family went to live in France and moved about it a great deal. She and her sister, when she was old enough, attended several different convent schools and both became expert bi-linguists—it helped them that their father was very bad at the French language. Jacqueline was living in Nice when she became eighteen and went to work at the unusual job—for a girl—of being a commercial traveller for a company which manufactured office equipment and furniture. It meant that she had to travel about a great deal and she gained an extensive knowledge of French cities, towns and railways. When France fell the family were not allowed to leave the country but Jacqueline and Eileen determined to escape somehow. By their own resources and with their own money they made their way to Portugal and reported to the British consul. He persuaded the captain of a British cargo ship to give the sisters a passage to Gibraltar,

'And he,' Jacqueline told me, 'had never had girls on board before. He was extremely nice and could not do enough for us. He gave us his own cabin for the voyage and loaded it with bunches of flowers.'

At Gibraltar the sisters were treated as refugees and put on a ship for Glasgow, where they might have been sent to a refugee camp if they had not insisted that they were British-born and on their way to a wealthy relative in London. In fact, when they came to London they went to stop with a friend of the family in Stamford Hill, a northern suburb. Then, together and separately, they badgered the recruiting offices of London for entry to the Services—it was mid-1942. Eileen was offered a job on a barrage-balloon site. Several of these sites on open spaces in and around London were manned by girls who raised a gas-filled balloon when an air-raid was imminent and winched it down again when the all-clear came through. (I was attached to the police in London at this time and one afternoon the girls reported that a visiting officer had disappeared mysteriously from the site. There was quite a flap for a time—then the girls reported that he had turned up again. They had trapped him accidentally under the balloon as they winched it down!) Eileen decided against balloons and Jacqueline was turned down by the Women's Royal Naval Reserve because she had no experience of driving in the black-out. They also registered for war service at the offices of Ministry of Labour and it was through this agency that SOE made contact with them.

The clerks at the Ministry of Labour had been instructed to send particulars of applicants who were bi-lingual or had any other special qualifications to the First Aid Nursing Yeomanry where they were vetted and, if the applications proved interesting the people concerned were interviewed. Jacqueline was surprised to receive a request one morning through the post to present herself for interview at an office in Whitehall where there might be employment for her.

The man she met there took her for a walk in the park and must have been very impressed for without more ado he asked her if she would like to go back to France. 'How?' she asked in astonishment. 'Oh by submarine or parachute,' he said. 'Parachute!' she echoed. But he told her that it was not so bad as it sounded and that she would be well-trained. Jacqueline made her mind up quickly too. 'All right. I'll go,' she said.

Then he explained that she would have to go through a rigorous testing and training period and that it was essential that she told nobody about what she was doing. She told him about her young sister and how difficult it would be not to tell her. He said not to worry; he would get Eileen a job also. They needed girls in Britain to become wireless operators and to code and de-code messages. He told Jacqueline to report to the headquarters of the FANYs where she was taught how to walk, salute and behave like a FANY officer and she was sent to Lillywhites, the outfitters in Piccadilly, to get measured for her uniform. She was told to say that she was driving officer's cars if anybody asked her. In the meantime Eileen had also joined, chosen to be a wireless operator, and had been sent to a training school. She was not at all convinced by Jacqueline's explanations and, in the course of her own job, soon discovered that girls were being sent to France. It was not long before she discovered the whole truth and began kicking up quite a fuss. In spite of Jacqueline's pleas SOE eventually found it necessary to accept Eileen as an agent also. But that was later.

Jacqueline went through the usual training in weapons, explosives and fieldcraft and was never quite happy that she was doing well. But she satisfied Colonel Buckmaster, although one of the training officers did not think her suitable. How wrong he was was very positively proven in the months that followed.

She and another FANY, Odette Churchill, George Cross, were the first two girls to be sent to the Ringway Parachute School for training. Parachuting was then very much a man's preserve—and only very tough men at that—so there was something like consternation in the instructor's school when the two girls turned up. A burly, incredulous sergeant stared at them and kept on repeating, 'You are lucky fellows—very lucky fellows indeed'. The girls had no idea what he meant, so they just took it that they were 'lucky fellows'.

In between jumps the two of them knitted socks furiously

for service in the field. They had been told that manufactured socks were dangerous because the Germans could easily distinguish between the French and the British weave, and the C.O. was heard to say that he hoped the influence of the ladies and their activities would have a humanizing effect on the troops.

Jacqueline was known there as 'Jackie red-socks' through her distinctive hose. In fact it helped in training for identification purposes as the instructors on the ground called out the traditional orders and instructions—including the hoary old joke which all the girls endured of being told to 'remember what their mothers told them' about keeping their knees together.

Back in London Jacqueline was introduced to a man named Maurice Southgate who, she was told, was to be her companion and C.O. in the field. If she did not like him she could say so and choose to go with another. In fact it would be difficult for anybody to dislike Maurice Southgate. He was a splendid officer whose integrity, courage and ingenuity in the field and later in German concentration camps earned him the highest possible opinions. Of British parentage he had been born and brought up in Paris, joined the British Army on the outbreak of war and was a survivor from the sinking of the troop ship *The Lancastria.* He was still an army officer when he joined SOE and was transferred as an officer to the Royal Air Force. Through some clerical delay he was, in fact, at one time an officer in both services and when stopping at his mother's house in South London used to go out in one or other of the uniforms. This confused a neighbour who said to his mother, 'I never see your two sons go out together'.

One October morning Maurice and Jacqueline left London for the aerodrome after an interview with Colonel Buckmaster. He always gave a present to the agents when they left—he presented her with a necklace and a gold watch and a hundred thousand francs, which she put in a belt around her body, for expenses in the field for herself. They set out for the first of five different abortive attempts to reach French soil. The first time there was no reception committee; the next time it was too foggy to drop; once again a reception committee was missing; the fourth time the engines of the aircraft failed and they did not even take off.

Eventually on 21st February 1943 they arrived over the dropping ground. They were told there was no reception committee but on this occasion they were instructed to drop blind, so Jacqueline, choosing to go first, jumped and made an excellent landing from five hundred feet. Sitting on the ground she watched the aeroplane turn and begin its journey home. It was a beautiful clear moonlit night. She folded her parachute before starting to look for Maurice when suddenly she saw two silhouettes in the moonlight—one of them was pointing a revolver at her. 'I felt it very unfair to be caught so quickly,' Jacqueline told me. 'I couldn't think what to do next. I just walked up and down trying to ignore the man and thinking to myself what I should say. I had done nothing wrong and my papers were in order—and then the man whispered my name. It was Maurice and the other silhouette was a stump of a tree'.

They hid their parachutes and threw away their maps and revolvers—without a reception committee they were on their own and if they were searched these things would immediately condemn them—and walked from 2 a.m. till 6 a.m. to the village where they had been directed to. Jacqueline, and Maurice himself, had another bad shock when Maurice spoke to the first man he met—in English. As it happened it was all right and the mistake helped them to be more careful in future. They bought tickets at the railway station in the village and boarding a train entered a carriage which was occupied by one other person, a German soldier. Jacqueline's heart jumped but they both sat down and began reading their papers—the soldier was not a bit interested in them and they reached Clermont Ferrand and arrived safely at a 'safe house'.

Thus began a long and busy career for both of them in which Jacqueline, posing as a commercial traveller, went backwards and forwards through her area conveying messages, finding dropping zones and organizing and attending reception committees, while Maurice organized arms training and widespread sabotage. Once he asked Jacqueline to take a message by train the following morning. She joined the train which started up, but got nowhere—the line had been blasted and it was evening before she returned home. She was very annoyed when Maurice apologetically explained that he had forgotten all about her message and had blown all the points along the line during the night. On another occasion Maurice earned something like a magician's reputation—as he was talking to a group of French workers a German aeroplane took off. As it gained height he said, 'I bet it's going to blow up.' And immediately afterwards it did! He did not explain to them he had placed a time bomb on it during the night.

After twelve months in the field Colonel Buckmaster felt that Jacqueline and Maurice should return to England for a well-deserved rest, and he instructed them to return, but they both said they would like to remain—especially as D-day was approaching. The Colonel agreed that Maurice might stay but he instructed Jacqueline to come back by a Lysander which was being sent over to drop two agents. Jacqueline met the Lysander but gave her seat up at the last minute to a French politician. The Colonel then sent an urgent order and even chalked on the side of the next Lysander to be sent 'Jacqueline MUST come'. So she returned. Maurice was betrayed shortly afterwards—the Germans had put a price of one million francs on his head and after the usual treatment was sent to Buchenwald concentration camp which he survived. After the war he returned to his interior decorating business in Paris.

Just before Jacqueline left France she had heard the dreadful news that her young sister Eileen had been captured by the Germans in the Paris area. As we have seen, Eileen eventually persuaded SOE to accept her and she was sent to France. She landed and joined a circuit near Paris as a wireless operator in March 1944. This circuit picked up a great amount of military and industrial intelligence which Eileen swiftly transmitted to London. It included the position of two thousand V-1 rockets which the RAF bombed. In between scheduled times she assisted reception committees and acted as a courier but one day whilst she was transmitting the German direction finders trapped her and she was caught at her set. They gave her a dreadful time, but did not succeed in discovering who she was. She stuck to her story that she was a French girl named Mademoiselle du Tort who was a bit of a scatterbrain and tomboy and who was helping the resistance for fun and excitement. They sent her to work in a factory in Germany and there they discovered her sabotaging the machinery and they shaved her hair, but they never tamed her. When the Americans reached German soil she escaped from the factory and made her way across country to their lines. They would not believe her when she said she was a British agent and put her in a cage with German women suspects. She endured a most unpleasant time until the British eventually caught up with her and flew her back to England.

Another young lady who served under Maurice Southgate was Pearl Witherington who came from Baldock in Hertfordshire, England. Pearl like most of the other women agents was decorated after the war and there was quite a controversy at the time because 'red tape' ordained that the decorations for girls who worked in the field should come from the civil not the military lists. Pearl was awarded the MBE (civil) so she sent it back explaining, 'I did nothing civil'. Eventually the authorities changed their minds and she accepted the MBE (military). In fact the Germans considered her so uncivil that they offered a million francs for information leading to her capture and posted bills to this effect all around the area where she was operating.

She was living in Paris with her mother and two younger sisters when war broke out and was working in the office of the British Air Attaché in Paris, where she met Maurice Southgate, and she was still in Paris when the triumphant Germans roared in there with their tanks and held victory parades in the historic streets. She had also met a young French officer named Henri Cornioley with whom she fell in love. He had been fighting the Germans and was captured by them when the French armies collapsed. In the midst of the tragedy that had befallen Europe Pearl's problems were acute. They were an English family due, at any moment, to be picked up and interned by the Germans. They determined to run for it, and taking as much as they could carry they set out from Paris on 9th December 1940 for the unoccupied zone of France. The day after they left the Germans called to arrest them.

'After having slipped through their hands the four of us boarded a train and left the Gare de Lyon station. We had no idea at all of how we could cross the demarcation line,' Pearl told me. 'But in the carriage we spoke to a man who said he was an escaped prisoner-of-war and had been free for some time and frequently crossed and re-crossed the line. We were not sure that we could trust him, but we had to take a chance and in the end he proved to be quite genuine. We followed him off the train at a small station at 4.30 a.m. It had been pouring with rain and the ground was muddy and slippery. We started out on our trek across country in the dead of night, not knowing where we were going. There was the man, with his bicycle, Mummy, Mimi, Jackie and myself. We splashed through a farm and Jackie lost her shoes in the mud—but we could not wait to find them because we had to be across the line by 6 a.m. to catch a bus to the nearest town. We met a German sentry and we all dived, face down, into a ditch. Mummy spread a rug she was carrying over the bicycle and he did not spot us as he passed by. We went on. When we got near the end of 'No Man's Land' our guide told us to wait and he went ahead to see if the coast was clear. It was and he came back and told us to run. Run! Our legs were giving way.'

But they managed it and caught the bus which took them towards Cherbourg. They remained there for three months, during which time Pearl worked with an escape group which was passing thousands of escaped prisoners-of-war and other refugees away from France and out of Hitler's clutches.

Then they re-started their own trek and eventually reached Lisbon where they boarded a ship to Greenock, in Scotland, and from there they reached London on 14th July 1941. Her two young sisters joined the Women's Auxiliary Air Force at once and Pearl rejoined the Air Ministry. She knew about the existence of SOE and again met Maurice Southgate who was already a member of it. She wanted to join too so she asked her chief, the Director of the Directorate of Allied Air Co-operation if he would help her. He was definite and abrupt—it was nonsense and he would not hear any more about it.

He should have known Pearl better—she went about it in her own way and through her own friends and was accepted. He was very annoyed and quite helpless to do anything about it when she turned up in his office one day in the uniform of a FANY officer!

After her course of training a woman officer of SOE said of her—'She was transformed into a self-reliant young woman, ready to assume authority. She had become a fine shot, and had acquired a good knowledge of weapons and tactics. She was a good-looking girl, tall and fair, with delicate features and had about her an air of calm and steadiness'.

Her friend Maurice Southgate had by this time been dropped into the field and was earning himself a great reputation as the chief of an important, vast and scattered sector in the centre of France. Hector, as he was known in the field, was also being diligently searched for by the Germans who had put an enormous price on his head. He had to be extremely careful and was, at the same time, extremely busy—he badly needed a courier, a competent and energetic one capable of assisting in every one of his several responsibilities, one who could remain calm and steady in the perilous circumstances. He was also much concerned about arranging co-operation with an important group of Maquis in his sector which was lead by a truculent and unfriendly colonel. Maurice needed a shrewd and diplomatic person to deal with him. London decided that Pearl filled the bill on all these counts. She had already done good work in the field, she had well impressed her tutors in training and she knew and trusted Maurice.

The truculent colonel was one of those French people, and there were, and still are, quite a few of them, who were suspicious of, and unwilling to co-operate with the British. Tradition dies hard and old historic wounds were still unhealed in the minds of a minority who continued to believe the old canard about 'Perfidious Albion' and that Britain was always ready, 'to fight to the last Frenchman'. Such people, however, accepted without demur the arms, explosives, supplies and funds that Allied aeroplanes dropped to the reception zones.

Pearl was parachuted in on 23rd September 1943. Vera Atkins had prepared a very special pleasant surprise for her but, owing to the vagaries of the wind, it went slightly wrong —but only slightly. Vera knew that Henri Cornioley, Pearl's fianceé, had escaped from the German prisoner-of-war camp and was working with the resistance in Maurice Southgate's sector so she arranged for him to be on the reception committee waiting for Pearl. At the last minute the winds changed and she had to be dropped at a different spot about ten miles from where Henri was impatiently waiting. He soon arrived at the right spot, however!

She was soon in the thick of the battle—taking messages, organizing moon drops, teaching arms drill and sabotaging—especially sabotaging. She was also making good progress with the crusty colonel. She quickly attained the position of being acknowledged and highly respected as a leader.

On 1st May 1944, she narrowly escaped being captured by the Germans. Maurice was not so lucky. They found out, by treachery or torture, where he was resting and took him away for interrogation. They got nothing out of him and after their usual methods had failed they sent him to Buchenwald concentration camp in Germany. He had the unusual honour of being gazetted for the Distinguished Service Order whilst still a prisoner there.

His arrest was a great catastrophe for SOE. D-day was imminent and it was particularly important to the invasion forces that rail communication in his sector should be completely disorganized. The main lines to Normandy, where the invasion was planned, ran through it. London decided to divide the sector in halves, and they instructed Pearl to assume the duties and responsibilities of Officer Commanding one half. She didn't argue, indeed, at the time she had no time to think much about it because she had a very urgent and important task to do. In doing it she very nearly got herself shot by mistake by another group of the Resistance. She had to pass on a vital message to London and had no wireless operator of her own. So, like Nancy Wake in another part of France, she mounted her bicycle and set out on a lone and uncomfortable ride to a faraway sector which, she had been told had transmission facilities. She knew nobody in this sector and there was nobody there who knew her—and it was a tense and dangerous time when Germans were very much on the alert and members of Resistance were conscious of the threat from spies and double-agents.

'I had no password and when I arrived there the man whose name I knew was out of town,' she told me. 'I was told to return later by an uneasy and suspicious woman.

'When I went back I had an immediate feeling that something was wrong by the expression on the woman's face. She just motioned me into another room where there was a man waiting. He questioned me closely and he did not trust me. Everytime he asked me if I knew so-and-so I had to answer "No". And when I asked him similar questions I got the same answer. Things were looking very bad so I decided to throw my last card. "Do you know Octave?" I asked. "No," he said. "Well, his real name is C— and he was caught and imprisoned a short time after I was dropped on his landing ground." To my utter relief he said he knew him and he accepted me'.

And four armed men stepped out from the adjoining room where they had been hiding. They were convinced that she was a spy and had decided to kill her. They handled the message to London for her and she rode back to her area where there was much vital work to be done. The night before D-day and for several days and nights afterwards the countryside resounded to the bangs of plastic explosive blowing sections of the railway lines to pieces. She became a specialist in the art and achieved the record number of eight hundred successful main-line attacks in the vital month of June.

The Das Reich Panzer SS Division were ordered to go to Normandy to reinforce the hard-pressed German army there. The Division had to forget the railway as a means of transport and use the roads. At every turn they were harassed, ambushed and fired upon—they had to fight every inch of the way against the wraith-like guerrilla forces who did what damage they could and then faded away into the impenetrable wild country. The once-reputable fighting division was driven to furious distraction and took a dreadful revenge when they perpetrated one of the most atrocious war crimes of the period.

Near the village of Oradour-sur-Vagnes one of their prominent officers was shot dead in a skirmish. The Germans surrounded the village and ordered all the men, old and disabled, because all the younger men were 'on the run' or fighting with the Maquis, into the village square where they massacred them with machine-gun fire. Then they drove the women and children into the church and set fire to it. Soldiers stood around the church shooting anybody who tried to run away. Seven hundred women and children died, but a few survived to describe the dreadful carnage. Whether the Germans knew it, or not, the village they chose was Oradour-sur-Glane which is fifteen miles away from Oradour-sur-Vagnes.

After the invasion had started Pearl's forces grew apace and more and more Allied aircraft came from England to drop the tools of war—arms, supplies, food, money. Day and night the work of arming and training went on until she had nearly two thousand capable soldiers in her command.

Once she led them in a pitched battle, which lasted for fourteen hours against two thousand five hundred Germans. During it she was with a small group which had been cut off by the Germans—and she dived into a field of ripe corn. She remained hidden there for eleven hours in the blazing sun while the Germans raked the field with fire.

'I had to be very careful how I moved,' she said. 'I watched the heads of corn above me, and when they were stirred by the breeze I moved a little nearer the edge of the field. If I had not waited until the wind moved the corn the Boche would have noted the movement and fired directly at the spot. They finally gave up and I got away'.

By the end of July her force had risen to three thousand five hundred men and was taken over by the official French army. During her command, apart from the damage done by sabotage, over a thousand Germans had been killed in four months and it had been largely responsible for forcing the surrender of a further twenty thousand.

After the war I met her in Paris with her husband Henri Cornioley and her daughter Claire. Maurice Southgate was also there, recovered from his experiences in Buchenwald, and getting on with his peace-time business of furniture designing.

7

'THE WIDOW' AND 'LITTLE PEGGY'

A familiar figure on the roads about Poitiers in south-west France during 1942 and 1943 was the reserved, soberly-dressed widow who was forever cycling about studying ancient monuments and interested in rocks—and suchlike. She had come to live in the district after the death of her husband to be away from the alarms and exertions of war-torn Paris, and to eke out her small pension on cheaper food. Even the police and the Germans got used to her—she minded her own business and took little interest in local activities.

In fact, the quiet 'little widow' was Lise de Baissac who had parachuted into France on the morning of 25th September 1942. There was another girl with her, Andrée Borrel, and they were the first of the women agents to arrive by parachute. Andrée, a courier, went off to the Paris area where after performing much valuable work she was captured by the Germans and eventually killed in Natzweiler concentration camp.

Lise was neither courier nor wireless operator. The instruction given to her before leaving London was simple, direct and indicative of the high regard and trust SOE placed in her—'Go to Poitiers and establish yourself,' she was told. She was exceptionally successful and, compared with some others, unspectacular which is, after all, the mark of the best agent. Her brother Claude was also an agent of remarkable ability in the field where, amongst other feats, he won the distinction of courting and marrying his courier, Mary Herbert.

Lise and Claude were working in Paris when France fell. They were British subjects who were born in Mauritius. Claude who would have had difficulty, because he was a man, in obtaining papers to leave France, made his own way to Gibraltar where he boarded a ship for England. Lise applied for her exit papers in the ordinary way and was granted them —she too made for Gibraltar and by coincidence, joined the same ship as her brother. In London they sought something to do in the Services and Claude, who knew somebody at SOE was accepted by that organization. He recommended that his sister should also be taken in but, at that time, SOE had not yet thought of using women in the field. They changed their minds a few months later, however, and sent for Lise. 'When they told me that they wanted me to be something like a spy I objected. Being a Mata Hari did not appeal to me at all,' Lise told me. 'However, they said that it was not really spying but merely going to France and organizing and doing what I could for the Allies, so I agreed'.

The organization had no real contacts in Poitiers at that time so they gave her the names of two people whom they believed to be sympathizers—one was a priest, the other an auctioneer. Lise who had never been in the town before approached the priest first and told him who she was. His cloth forbade him from active participation with the resistance but he was very helpful and gave her the names of people whom she could trust; the auctioneer could and did help a great deal.

Lise found herself lodgings in her new name of Madame Eileen Brisse—an old family name—and settled down quietly to establish her identity as a harmless local nonentity. SOE wanted her to become an unobtrusive expert on local conditions, to learn all she could about the rationing system and rationing books, about food shortages, railway conditions, movement restrictions, passes and permits. Her accumulated and up-to-date knowledge would be invaluable to new agents. It would prevent them from making mistakes with ration books or producing permits and passes which had become obsolete.

As she cycled about Lise found and noted suitable grounds for parachute drops and built up gradually a circle of trustworthy and loyal helpers. Two months after she had settled in she heard on her wireless set that a new agent was to be dropped in her area and she was on the ground to meet him. She took him to her house and filled him in with all the details of contemporary conditions. She advised him on train times and conditions and saw him off next day to the part of France in which he was going to operate. For the next eleven months her work consisted mainly of such work—she became the reception officer for agents, and she also arranged for agents and other important individuals to be picked up and taken back to Britain. During the periods of the full moon Lise slept little. Every night men and materials were arriving or others had to be dispatched. She had to help in manhandling the containers, and arranging the safe disposal of the supplies and arms.

In August 1943 SOE in London had wind of a coming surge of Gestapo activity in her area. Treachery was suspected. She was ordered to return to London and she did so by Lysander. After she left there was a wide swoop on resistance groups in the area and several, including her auctioneer friend whom they killed, were arrested.

She left on 15th August and, again by coincidence, her brother Claude was on the same aircraft. He had been operating in an adjacent sector and had, indeed, on a number of occasions given Lise support—especially, when some of the French patriots had been doubtful about Lise's ability, because she was a woman.

Second Mission.

Back in England Lise had a well-deserved rest and was then sent on a refresher course at the training establishments and to the parachute school, where she broke a leg in a practice jump. 'I was too confident. I thought I knew everything but I didn't,' she said. This delayed her return to active service and it was April 1944 before she was passed fit.

D-day was very near then and the resistance, especially in the areas near the Cherbourg peninsula, were being placed in a state of immediate readiness. Claude, her brother, one of the most experienced and daring of the agents, had been sent to Normandy to organize the support for the landings and Lise asked to be sent there as well as his assistant. SOE agreed and she was sent over by Lysander. Once more she became a 'widow', this time under the name of Madame Janet Bouville but now she played a more active role. When Claude had to travel she took over command of his area and spent a great deal of time as an arms instructor. On the eve of D-day she was heavily engaged with groups demolishing railway lines and disrupting communications.

After D-day in the village where she lodged she saw keen and disciplined German troops moving to the front to stem the allied advance. Later she watched them returning as demoralized stragglers. In retreat they were a far greater threat to the French people in the towns and villages through which they passed. Lise found a room at the back of the school-house where she lived as a refugee but worked as an intelligence officer collecting and passing on information on the movement of the enemy troops.

Then the Germans took over the front of the school-house as their local headquarters and for a time they did not disturb her. German dispatch-riders used to come to the front of the school with their messages and reports; resistance messengers used to come to the back of the house to hand Lise theirs. Sometimes she caught a glimpse of the campaign maps on the walls of the German quarters and noted the disposition of the flags giving the German positions.

One day she was sure that it was all up. The German C.O. saw her approaching. He called her and told her that he wanted to take over the whole of the school—she must remove her bedding at once and get out. Lise hurried to the back and went in to find German soldiers already in possession. They had scattered her belongings all over the place—including the parachute silk which she had been using as a bed. They were sitting on it—'I was very scared but I felt there was nothing I could do except to remain calm and dignified as a "widow" should and demand my sheets back. They gave them to me without a word,' said Lise.

The bicycle played a very important part in the work of the Resistance and they were very scarce and expensive. In retreat the Germans were also very anxious to lay their hands on any they could find and one day a German soldier stopped her and attempted to take her precious means of transport. The 'widow' bridled immediately and in high indignation said that she knew his C.O. and that she would go immediately to the schoolhouse to report. The soldier thought better of it and walked away, swearing at her.

American troops were now advancing towards the area and Lise and her assistants were sending them frequent reports on the enemy movements. Through these reports the Americans were enabled to make constant and telling attacks.

One day the Germans packed up and left the village. Two hours later the first of the Americans arrived to liberate the area. They received the surprise of their lives. There waiting for them in the village square was FANY Captain Lise de Baissac in her smart military uniform and pips awaiting them! Lise, with noble optimism on the success of the allied invasion, had brought her uniform with her on the second mission and buried it safely to await the coming of the liberators. The villagers also were amazed to find that the 'widow' was a British officer and even more so when the Americans handed over control to her and passed on. She was very busy again now mopping up the arms and ammunition which she had stored around the countryside and locating the lonely graves where the men and women of the Resistance had been interred. She also became judge and jury for the villagers who were rounding up the people who had collaborated with the enemy.

After the war Lise worked in London with the BBC. She was a programme assistant on the Overseas service, where she translated news from English into French and also acted as a news reader. Later she married a Monsieur Villameur and went to live in France.

Discussing her life in the field Lise said, 'Films and novels have made people think of an agent's work as glamorous. But believe me, our job was, above all, sheer hard work. What was needed was cold-blooded efficiency for long weary months rather than any burst of heroism. Looking back I find my strongest emotion was acute loneliness—the loneliness of a secret life. Even the relief of talking to other agents was the rarest luxury—for our own safety we were only supposed to contact one another when strictly necessary'.

The only thrill of her work which Lise admitted was the sensation of parachute jumping. 'I love all sport but parachuting is the greatest fun of all.'

The only honour she claimed for herself was that she was still alive and well. 'They did not catch me. In that rather serious game of hide-and-seek I won. I am rather proud of that.'

Colonel Buckmaster talking about her after the war said, 'Lise is one of the bravest women I have ever known. Her war record was exceptional'.

On 31st October 1942 Mary Herbert arrived by felucca on the Mediterranean coast of France with two other girls, Odette Churchill G.C. and forty-eight-year old Madame Le Chene. Mary was on her way to Bordeaux where she was to work as courier for Claude de Baissac—and plenty she had to do because he was always one of the most active and aggressive of agents. They found time, however, to fall in love and Colonel Buckmaster received a message which when de-coded read, 'Am going to marry Mary—please put your banns up in any Church you can'. This was done and a year afterwards another message arrived: 'Mary is going to have baby—please send suitable gear'.

Vera Atkins went shopping then, and the FANYs in the coding rooms and on the wireless sets started knitting baby clothes. The Germans would have been puzzled if they had captured one container which was dropped at the next parachutage—it was packed with napkins, safety-pins, gripe water and all kinds and colours of baby wear. It was a little boy.

Peggy Knight is a diminutive figure, five feet tall, very slim but a bundle of energy, vivacious, ready to smile and always a very popular girl but, nevertheless, unassuming and modest. She is now Mrs Margery Smith, married to an ex-submariner and the mother of two fine sons. It is difficult to explain how she survived the war—she was sought by the Germans, questioned by them, even entertained by them. She shot them and blasted them with bombs and she survived when her group was infiltrated and nearly destroyed by German spies who became prominent and influential members of it. Her father was a British officer who lived in Paris after the First World War. Peggy lived in France until she was sixteen, so becoming a first class bi-linguist. Then the family returned to live in the county of Kent in southern England where she attended school at Canterbury. She left to become a shorthand-typist and in 1943, when she was twenty-three joined the Women's Auxiliary Air Force. A year afterwards she was discharged as medically unfit—she had survived a serious bout of pneumonia. So she became a shorthand-typist again with a firm of engineers who had offices in the City of London.

One evening in February 1944 Peggy and friends from her office went to the lounge of a tavern in the Strand, London, to celebrate the birthday of one of the girls. During an interval in the conversation Peggy heard a slight plop as a book slipped off an adjoining table on to the floor and she instinctively stooped and picked the book up, as she replaced it on the table she involuntarily read the title aloud—it was in French. The owner of the book was a British officer who said 'Thank you,' and then added 'Your French accent is very good'. Peggy replied, 'It ought to be, I was sixteen years in Paris,' and so started a conversation which ended with Peggy floating down to the soil of France a few short months later. The officer and herself chatted as Peggy's friends talked amongst themselves and Peggy explained how boring the job of shorthand-typist can be. When she said that he suggested that she should join one of the various women's corps so she told him about her discharge. Eventually he said he might possibly be able to help her if she cared to phone him at the number he gave her. Peggy phoned next morning and saw him on a few further occasions when he talked about everything except the job that he had hinted at. After a few weeks she received a letter inviting her to present herself at a room in Whitehall. She went but she still had not guessed what it was about. A pleasant-faced man with an Irish accent questioned her closely and for a very long time, but it seemed to Peggy then that he knew most of the answers already. Then he said, 'Would you be prepared to accept a job which will take you into enemy-occupied France and may well lead to your capture and death by the Gestapo?'

'Certainly,' said Peggy.

There was an urgent need then for couriers and no time was lost in Peggy's training. Most of the girls had about six months training, Peggy was given only three weeks. Instead of the usual five practice jumps at the parachute school Peggy did one. She returned to London on a Saturday to spend a restful weekend after her strenuous training but was suddenly recalled the same afternoon and told to be ready to leave for France in an hour's time.

She was given the usual complete set of papers to prove that her name was now Marguerite Chauvin, an orphan, working as a shorthand-typist. She was also handed ten thousand francs and a packet of tablets which would help to fight off sleep in times of emergency, and an L (for lethal) tablet in case she should choose to die rather than face torture. When Peggy learned what it was for she realized, if she did not before, the full dangers of her mission. She was told that it would guarantee her own death in a matter of seconds.

That afternoon the hustling went on and it was only in the car on the way to the aerodrome that she was introduced to her collegue Noel who was to drop with her. At the aerodrome Peggy and Noel went through the usual last-minute scrutiny, tried out their revolvers, entered an American plane and flew into the night sky. They were the first agents to be taken from Great Britain to France in an American plane. The darkness of blacked-out England gave way to the silvery brilliance of the English Channel and as she watched the shadows of Britain's shores recede Peggy began to feel frightened and wish that she had never come in contact with the organization. But there was no turning back and soon they were amidst the welcoming bursts of German flak. About 1 a.m. they were in the vicinity of their dropping area in Burgundy near to the river Yonne. The Reception Committee's signal was clearly picked out and at the word of command from a member of the crew Peggy launched herself for her second parachute jump and landed perfectly. Her companion Noel followed but was not so fortunate, he had to be extricated from the branches of a tall tree.

The group who received them had not expected any 'bods' that night—they certainly did not expect a diminutive little girl but they hurriedly made some arrangements and took them both to a farm near a village. News soon spread that a tiny little Englishwoman had arrived and next day there was a pilgrimage of curious villagers to gaze at the new arrivals. Such publicity was quite contrary to the rules of security and the 'bods' were not a little worried at their notoriety. Next night to their relief they were escorted to a farm much further away where they had to remain a week in hiding before arrangements to fit them into a group were concluded. Living in a farm outhouse is not much fun especially when one begins to itch all over but it served for Peggy as an introduction to very uncomfortable work she was going to do. It was decided that she should stay where she was and commence her work immediately. Her sector was expected to become a very important one as the Germans were expected to retreat to there as soon as the invasion had commenced, which in fact they did.

This made it necessary for a very large amount of arms and ammunition to be dropped there and Peggy now spent most of her nights helping to collect and bury the arms and equipment and most of her days cycling about, ostensibly looking for a job but really conveying messages to out-of-the-way members of the group. One morning shortly after her arrival and when she had been working all night at an arms drop she was told to go to Paris to pick up a wireless transmitting set. As she sat in the corner of a crowded compartment in a train, which was forced to stop frequently through bomb damage and sabotage, she dozed off and suddenly woke with a start to find all eyes in the compartment fixed on her. She had been dreaming about England and had been talking in her sleep—in English! It was a very worried Mademoiselle Chauvin who waited for the train to stop at the Paris terminus. Then she nipped smartly out before the train came to a final stop and quickly lost herself in the crowds.

She went straight to the address which she had been given but she was not to know that she had arrived at a time when the Gestapo were playing havoc with the Paris sector and everybody connected with the resistance was in hourly fear of betrayal and arrest. The woman who answered her knock was in a highly nervous state and told Peggy to get out of the neighbourhood at once—a Gestapo swoop was imminent. She gave Peggy another address to go to but added that it too was highly dangerous. But Peggy did not have much choice and she was almost completely exhausted from the travelling so she went to the other address where, when she had identified herself, she was allowed to sleep.

Next morning she remembered an old school-friend who might still be living in Paris and she went to the house. The girl was delighted to see her and welcomed her but then the girl remembered that Peggy was supposed to be in England and suddenly became appalled when she guessed that Peggy was some kind of secret agent for the Resistance. The girl's panic was not, however, so much on her own part but because her mother, an old lady, was very ill and nervous and would have probably died of fright if she knew they were sheltering a secret agent. Her friend smuggled her upstairs to the attic where Peggy spent an uncomfortable but safe night and left smartly next morning. She had learned that the house next door was the Gestapo Headquarters!

Peggy's instructions were to go to a certain seat in the Jardin de Tuilleries and wait there until another agent sat down and handed her a parcel containing the wireless set. She sat there perfectly at ease until a German Army officer passed by and gave her an admiring glance. Then he retraced his footsteps, sat down beside her and started to engage her in conversation. She did not know the other agent, who was due to arrive at any moment, and this might lead to disaster or, at least, to the breaking of the secret assignation. Then the Air Raid warning went and the German officer suggested that she went with him to the air raid shelter at his hotel. Peggy had no alternative but to agree. She kept him in conversation there about his magnificent Luger pistol and he told her that it was the end of his leave in Paris and that his train was shortly due out. When the 'All Clear' sounded Peggy went with him to the railway station and stood waving her handkerchief until the train disappeared in the distance. She hurried back to the park bench and met her contact, one of the most celebrated of the Resistance leaders who was subsequently captured and died in Belsen Concentration Camp.

She returned to her sector without incident, but to discover a most disturbing state of affairs. The whole of the Group was seething with dissatisfaction and suspicion. The local leader of the Maquis was executed by his own men and Peggy, herself, was in grave danger of death. She did not know till long afterwards how near she was to a sudden execution as the result of the poison which had been sown by a double-agent, but eventually the crisis subsided. It was a most disturbing and dangerous period when nobody had any idea who the traitor was. They were in constant fear of Gestapo swoops and when one came Peggy and her friends jumped from a back window into a deep river and waded to the further bank where they lay all day in their sodden clothes.

At nightfall they walked ten miles to a safe house and learned next day that it was D-day—the invasion had started. Peggy now took to the woods with a group of Maquis, taught them the use of the weapons, and took her place nightly in marauding missions. The railway lines from Marseilles to Paris passed through their sector and provided them with an important, obvious and frequent target. At night she went with her friends carrying plastic explosives, creeping past farmhouses to avoid the noisy watch-dogs, throwing themselves into the roadside ditches as German lorries drove past and worming their way past German sentries to the permanent way. After attaching the little packets with time fuses to the vital spots they wormed their way back to a safe distance, waited for the sound of the explosives and counted them to find out if there had been any duds. For one of these actions little Peggy was awarded the Croix de Guerre.

The Maquis lived in a deserted farmhouse and one day an escaped British Officer, Captain Thompson, who had escaped from a German prisoner-of-war camp arrived. He helped in training and he took his turns at sentry duty and the saboteur operations. One night Captain Thompson and Peggy were doing their normal turn of sentry duty around the farmhouse where their companions slept when they heard a shot in the distance. Thompson went to reconnoitre whilst Peggy warned her companions of the danger. Thompson returned to report that there were about seven hundred Germans approaching in what appeared to be a surrounding movement of the farmhouse. The group bundled up as much arms and ammunition as they could carry and ran for it. Peggy and a Frenchman made their way to the thickest part of the woods and laid low. The Germans made contact with the others and a minor engagement developed with bullets and mortar shells exploding all over the place. The rest of the night and most of the following day the shooting went on whilst Peggy and her companion quietly hid—when the shooting ceased they set out to walk more than twenty miles to another safe house.

Peggy spent most of her time during the day cycling about from farm to farm and house to house making the assignations for after-dusk forays—by day she was a little innocent French girl and at night became a determined, courageous, soldier of the Underground. She had many unpleasant jobs to do—one dark night she wielded her spade in the depth of a wood to dig up a dead body which had been buried a week before. Some papers had subsequently been missed and it was thought that they might be on the corpse.

On another occasion it became essential to execute a double-agent. That is a man who was working for the Germans but had infiltrated into an Underground group. There were double agents on both sides, of course, but their fate was swift and sure when their true allegiance leaked out. In this case it was a chemist who was to be executed. Peggy and companions drove to the shop, and one of them entered whilst Peggy stood with her sten gun outside the door. The chemist was very much on the alert and seeing the armed man entering drew a revolver and fired immediately, seriously wounding Peggy's companion. She rushed into the shop with her Sten gun blazing, the chemist escaped through the back and Peggy and another of the Group carried their wounded comrade back to the car, he died almost immediately. By this time the sound of the shots had aroused the Germans; they were very lucky to escape the hail of bullets which followed them as they drove away.

The group received information that a convoy of German lorries was due to pass through their area with sorely-needed supplies for the front line. Peggy cycled furiously to inform her scattered group. She was with nineteen of them as they lay in ambush later that evening, and from a distance of twenty-five yards she pumped bullets into the bonnets of the lorries. The action did not last long; the Germans threw their arms away and surrendered.

When the Germans started retreating an American Liaison officer, a Major Colby was dropped to her area. His job was to liaise between the Underground Army and the Americans who were shortly expected. It became imperative to find out where the American Army was and Peggy was sent off on her bicycle to make her way through the German front line and establish contact. She was stopped and questioned. She said she was suffering from a raging toothache and was on her way to a dentist. The Germans were sympathetic but they could not help, they told her to return home as it was dangerous for civilians to be about. Having no success in the day-time Peggy decided to try a quick dash through the German lines after dark. She managed to get hold of one of the few cars available and a driver and one pitch black night without headlights, they penetrated the German posts and made contact with the Americans. At the American headquarters they gave all the information they could and then the American Colonel asked them if they would be kind enough to return through the German lines and obtain some information about a German tank concentration which he suspected to be a few miles from the forward position.

So Peggy and her driver once more set out to cross through the Germans. With the windscreen open and both of them peering into the inky blackness they accomplished this, obtaining the required information and returned once again to the American headquarters. Then they set out on their journey home—they were not so lucky this time. Rounding a bend they saw a German convoy nearly but not quite blocking the road in front. It was too late to turn back, the convoy was stopped and Germans were standing about in groups.

The driver decided that he was going to try to burst through—Peggy gathered three hand grenades. As the car speeded at the surprised Germans Peggy slung the hand grenades amongst them and they were past and away to a safe distance before the Germans had recovered from the effects of the bombs. They reached home without further incident.

Within a week the American First Army was in control of the sector but Peggy's work had not finished. She now spent her time cycling through the German lines to collect information on their troop dispersals and concentrations on behalf of the American Army. On one of these journeys she heard about a pocket of British SAS troops who were cut off in a remote part of the country and she made her way to them. She had some difficulty in approaching their position as they were very much on the alert and when she was eventually allowed into their position had even more difficulty in persuading them that she was a British girl and member of the First Aid Nursing Yeomanry. The SAS were expecting to be attacked by a German force then occupying a town some miles distant and Peggy volunteered to visit the town to find out something of the strength of the enemy forces. She was stopped by a German sentry as she neared the approaches to the town but he let her pass when she explained about her terrible toothache; further on an NCO directed her to an officer's quarters. The officer was sympathetic but could not help much; he insisted, however, that she should swallow two of his aspirins and drink a cup of hot strong coffee. He sent her back the way she had come in—during the conversation Peggy gathered that the German force amounted to about six hundred men and three tanks. She returned with that information to the SAS group. Then the Americans too passed on through her area and war receded. Her work there was done, so Peggy set off for Paris

—not in a luxurious military car but by hitch-hiking. From Paris Peggy was sent back to England which she reached on 13th September 1944.

The little girl who had been rushed through her training, skimped her parachuting, been invalided out of the RAF and was scared stiff going to France was awarded the rare American Medal of Freedom, the French Croix de Guerre and the British MBE.

8

VIOLETTE, GEORGE CROSS

When Nancy Wake, the irreverent irrepressible Australian girl, was sent on an explosives course—how to mix, place and detonate—during her initial training she met and took an immediate 'shine' to a kindred spirit, a slim, beautiful, high-spirited twenty-two-year-old girl named Violette Szabo. They shared a room, proved to be apt and interested pupils during working hours and boisterous, mischievous and tireless in the off-duty hours.

The pupils and staff were all bursting with health and energy and inevitably a good amount of practical joking went on. There was the occasion when the two girls suddenly fell on one of their instructors, who had been strict with them during lessons, determined to de-bag him. A strenuous battle ensued in which the contestants used most of the holds and grips they had been taught in unarmed combat, and spectators watched with professional interest. He proved no match for the girls and retired from the fray in his striped underpants.

On another occasion the two girls felt slighted because they had not been invited to a staff party. In retaliation they went to the C.O.'s room and stripped it of furniture, bedding, carpet and clothes. When the C.O. returned he thought he had come to the wrong room so he re-checked and examined the only piece of evidence left—his own tin hat. He quickly realized who the culprits were and went to the girl's room to do something about it. They had barricaded themselves in!

A few short weeks afterwards Violette, carrying identity papers which stated that she was a commercial secretary living in Le Havre, travelled by herself into the most dangerous forbidden zone of the Atlantic wall of France. It was her first mission and brilliantly carried out.

Her father was an Englishman, Charles Bushell, who had met and married an attractive Frenchwoman when he was serving in France during the First World War. The family were living in Paris when Violette was born on 26 June 1921. She spent many years there and became a fluent bi-linguist. Then they moved to Brixton, a south-west suburb of London, where Violette went to school and on leaving, became a hairdresser's assistant. From hairdressing she drifted to becoming an assistant in the Brixton Bon Marché, a large departmental store and at one time also worked as an assistant in the local branch of Woolworth's stores. She was a tomboy from childhood, loved games, was a keen cyclist and a very good gymnast. She had no interest in politics or similar affairs and did not take the war seriously when it started. She did, however, think of joining one of the Services but a girl friend suggested the Land Army, a regiment of girls who helped farmers—and they both joined and spent some pleasant weeks picking strawberries. When France fell the tragedy of the war was brought home to the family, especially to the mother, and Violette decided to join a more active service and returned home. She was at home on Bastille day, 14th July, when a parade of the Free French Army was due to take place in London. Her mother thought it would be a good idea if they invited one of the troops home for dinner—the soldiers were strangers in England and would probably enjoy meeting somebody who could speak their language. She suggested that Violette should go to the parade and find one. Violette and her girl friend went and afterwards a handsome and well-built young officer wearing the eye-catching uniform of the French Foreign Legion spotted the attractive Violette and introduced himself. He was Etienne Michel René Szabo, a professional soldier who had seen much active service in North Africa, Norway and other European countries. He was delighted to accept the invitation to dinner; they fell in love and were married five weeks afterwards, on 21st August at a Registry Office in Aldershot. The ceremony was interrupted by an air-raid which obliged the couple and their friends to sit in an air-raid shelter for two hours. They had a honeymoon which lasted only a few days because he had to sail with his regiment to North Africa. She saw him only once again—for a week's holiday in Liverpool to where he had been sent for a rest. After he flew back to Cairo Violette joined the ATS, the women's branch of the British Army, and was posted to an anti-aircraft unit which defended the Liverpool area. In April 1942 she had to leave because she was going to have a baby which was born on 8th June at St Mary's Hospital, Paddington, London. It was a little girl whom Violette christened Tania. When Tania was old enough Violette used to leave her in her mother's care and work in a war factory near Brixton. For a time she was in regular correspondence with her husband but then his letters stopped and Violette became worried and tried without success to get news of him at the Free French Headquarters in London. Eventually bad news arrived—he had been killed whilst advancing against the Germans at El Alamein.

Violette took it very badly and was very dejected for a time. It not only shocked her but it intensified the hatred she felt against the people responsible for it as well as for all the terror, destruction and horror they had spread throughout Europe.

Out of the blue a letter arrived which invited her to an interview in an office in Whitehall. She had no idea what it was about but, curious—though not very interested, she decided to go. She was not to know that the War Office had circularized Army units asking for particulars of bi-lingual personnel and that her name had been sent to SOE. The Department's recruiting officer Captain Selwyn Jepson, decided to see her and he was impressed when he met her. As usual he mentioned that there was a job available which might lead to an active role in the war. She immediately became interested and when he said that it might even lead to service in France she became enthusiastic. It was, it seemed, just what she was looking for. Certainly she was ready and would love to go to France.

It was the Captain who became a little cagey then. He liked keenness but this was going a little far—he wondered if she would, after all, be suitable for the very dull, dangerous and highly confidential work of a secret agent. He told her to go away and think about it—he wanted time to think about her himself! She went away slightly disappointed that she had not got the job on the spot—and she had carefully avoided mentioning her baby in case it went against her. She was on the phone next morning to know if she was in! She had to wait impatiently for more than a week before she was asked to return for another interview when she was delighted to hear that she had been selected for training—on trial.

SOE rarely had a more willing pupil. Her quick intelligence, fitness and enthusiasm enabled her to scamper through tests, she was outstanding at weapon training and became an expert with the Bren and Sten guns. She told her training officer Peggy Minchin, that she just wanted some Germans to fight and that she would be happy to die if she could take some of them with her. Unfortunately, she twisted her ankle badly whilst at the parachute training school and had to rest it for a month. It was never very strong afterwards.

The area in France adjoining the Atlantic ocean near the Cherbourg peninsula was of vital importance to the Allies because it was about there they intended to invade. It was equally vital to the Germans because they expected that it would, in fact, be the invasion area and consequently their intelligence services were extremely alert and their security services, soldiers and police were very much on their toes. It was to this area that Violette and her officer Captain Charles Staunton were ordered to go. They were to help ensure that the area would be thoroughly disrupted for the Germans when the invasion started. They were ready to leave when the grievous news arrived that the Germans had swooped successfully on the Resistance in the area and completely shattered it—most of the members had been arrested and deported to Germany. The Gestapo were in full control and, they were told, it would be madness to go. Of course. But now it became more urgent than ever for the Allies to have detailed information about what had happened, how many useful sympathizers were left and how and when a new Resistance circuit could be started. Somebody had to go—so Violette went. Staunton could not go—he had organized the old circuit and the Germans knew all about him. His picture decorated thousands of posters pasted all over the area offering a reward for information leading to his capture.

They were landed by Lysander on an air-strip near Paris on 6th April 1944, were safely picked up by the reception committee and lodged in a safe house in Paris. A few days later Violette, now Mademoiselle Corrine Reine Leroy, left by train for her two-hour journey to Rouen. She had no definite, trustworthy contacts but Staunton told her the names and addresses of a few people he trusted and hoped had not been scooped up by the Germans. She would have to be exceedingly careful; no doubt they had been betrayed and the traitor might still be posing as a sympathizer. She would be very much on her own and would have to make her own decisions and use her own initiative and intuition. She had to memorize all she was told; it would be too dangerous to have written evidence.

She left Paris in a train packed with soldiers returning to their units from leave. She was the only civilian in a carriage occupied by German officers. She smoked their cigarettes and carried on a desultory conversation with them.

In Rouen she carried out her instructions to the letter, delicately picked up the threads and moved from sympathizer to sympathizer. She remained there for two weeks and had several brushes with the Germans. They arrested her twice, once holding her in a police station for four hours—but she talked her way out and returned to Paris with a full and accurate report of conditions. She brought Staunton back one of the posters on which his photo appeared.

They returned to England by Lysander immediately but not before Violette had visited the stores of Paris and bought gifts for her friends and a frock for Tania.

Second Mission

In London Violette had five weeks rest before her next mission. She spent a great deal of time with her little daughter, and also found time to spend evenings dining with friends in some of London's restaurants and clubs.

One evening in June she drove, once again with Vera Atkins, to an aerodrome in Bedfordshire. Describing her afterwards, Vera said she was calm, composed, beautiful and made a striking picture. She was alive with health and good spirits. On the day after D-day 7th June she and Staunton jumped from an American Liberator aircraft to a Maquis group in south-west France near Limoges. Their task this time was to help organize the Maquis and urge and assist them to aggressive activity. Important lines of communication ran through the area and these should be put out of action, and the Germans harried and attacked, so that the reinforcements could not get through to the Germans trying to stem the Allied advance. Staunton lost no time in impressing the urgency for action upon the Maquis. His most important assistant then was an officer named Anastasia who had been there for months and knew all about local conditions, numbers and location of adjacent groups. They decided that all these groups should be alerted at once and Violette was deputed to visit them—Anastasia was to drive her to the first one. Before they left, Staunton told Violette that it was of the utmost importance that Anastasia returned safely—his knowledge was vital.

As Anastasia and Violette drove to the first group they ran into an advance party of thirty men of an SS infantry regiment who were already on their way to reinforce the German divisions. They left the car and ran for it—the Germans fired and Violette was hit in the arm, but she continued to run and turn and fire bursts from her sten gun at the pursuers. Then her weak ankle gave way and Anastasia went to assist her—she told him to leave her and escape. She would remain and try to hold them off. Anastasia argued but she insisted, told him that it was important that *he* got away and standing up emptied her magazine at the Germans who had now been joined by four hundred troops. Anastasia ran on and hid himself in a heap of firewood that was beside a road. She continued to fire until her ammunition was exhausted and the Germans closed in and took her biting and kicking to an officer who stood then by the firewood in which Anastasia was hiding. The officer offered her a cigarette—she spat in his face.

They did not find Anastasia but they took her to a jail in Limoges. It is not known for certain how many Germans were killed or wounded by Violette's covering fire—the Germans took all casualties with them. Every day for a week she limped, guarded by Germans, from the jail to the Gestapo offices in the town where she was interrogated for hours, but not ill-treated. They got nothing out of her and sent her to the notorious prison at Fresnes near Paris. Later, as we shall see, Violette had an opportunity of speaking with a British Officer when they were on their way to concentration camps. He survived the war and reported what she had told him to SOE. From Fresnes she was taken on several occasions to the Gestapo Headquarters in Paris for further questioning and when she refused to reveal any details of her work or her organization was brutally tortured. She did not subsequently dwell on this and was reluctant to speak about it but it is certain that when she returned from the Gestapo on the last occasion she spent some days in bed at Fresnes in severe pain—one of the days was her twenty-third birthday!

In August 1944 when the Allies were approaching Paris the Germans evacuated their prisoners and deported them to prisons and concentration caps in Germany. Violette was one of twelve women who were chained in pairs and loaded aboard a train for a nightmare journey that lasted a week. She met two other SOE women agents on the train—she was chained to one of them—and there were several SOE men officers chained in the next compartment—including a good friend of hers named Harry Peuleve.

One girl was Denise Bloch, a Jewess who went under the name of Danielle Williams. She had worked with the Resistance in France before escaping to Britain and joining SOE. After training she returned to the Paris Sector by Lysander on 3rd March 1944, to act as courier for Robert Benoist. She carried out much useful work until the group was betrayed in Paris on 19th June 1944. The Gestapo raided one of the Benoist hide-outs on the day afterwards and captured Denise.

The other girl was Lilian Rolfe, a tall dark girl whose father was English and her mother French. She had been brought up in Brazil but was living in Woking, Surrey when she joined SOE. She arrived in the field on 6th April 1944 to act as wireless operator to George Williams, a British officer in charge of a circuit at Orleans. He was arrested in June 1944 and she continued to operate for a month until she was 'accidentally' captured when a group of Germans called at a house where she was staying on a matter not at all connected with her work, but they saw and questioned her and took her into custody. She had been but four months in France.

The train carrying the agents was attacked by British fighters. During the attack the Germans left the train and set up machine-gun posts to try to defend themselves and during this period Violette, with the other girl chained to her, dragged herself through the corridor with bottles of water for the men agents who were going mad with thirst. Seventeen of the Germans were killed by the air attack, and the train was put out of commission. That night the prisoners were lodged in nearby stables, and it was then that Harry Peuleve and Violette managed to have their last conversation. Jack-booted women guards wielding whips met the girls when they arrived at the concentration camp at Ravensbruck, about fifty miles north of Berlin. Amongst the several thousand unfortunate women there when they arrived were ex-secretary Yvonne Baseden, Yvonne Rudellar and Cecily Lefort, but they never came across each other.

Violette, Denise and Lilian shared the same miserable bunk in a dreadful hut which was infested with lice and stank of death and corruption. They were forced to work from dawn to dusk building roads, or working in the fields or war factories. Even in these awful conditions Violette was cheerful and kept her spirit of adventure—twice she was caught trying to escape and sent to solitary confinement; once she was given ten strokes of the birch. The three of them were sent to a site three hundred miles away where in severe wintry conditions they were forced to fell trees and prepare the land for an aerodrome, and then a few months before the German surrender they were sent back to Ravensbruck.

Nothing certain was known about what happened to them then until Vera Atkins travelled to Germany as soon after the end of hostilities as she could to try and trace her friends, the girls she had seen off to France. For many weeks she searched the prisons and camps where the war criminals were detained and interviewed hundreds who had been connected with the concentration camps. In the end she built up a great dossier of facts and evidence which was used at the subsequent trials. Amongst the men she questioned was Johann Schwarzhuber who had been the Ravensbruck second-in-command. He was hanged.

His statement given to Vera read:

'... One evening, towards 1900 hours they (Lilian, Danielle, Violette) were called out and taken to the cemetery yard by the crematorium. Camp Commandant Suhren made these arrangements. He read out the order for their shooting ... I was myself present.

'The shooting was done by Schult with a small calibre gun through the back of the neck. They were brought forward singly by Corporal Schenk. Death was certified by Dr K Trommer. The corpses were removed singly by internees who were employed in the crematorium, and burnt. The clothes were burnt with the bodies.

'I accompanied the three women in the crematorium yard. A female overseer was also present and was sent back when we reached the crematorium. Zappe stood guard over them while they were waiting to be shot.

'All three were very brave and I was deeply moved, Suhren was also impressed by the bearing of these women. He was annoyed that the Gestapo did not themselves carry out these shootings ...'

9

THE COUNTESS

Ann Marie Walters counted herself lucky to reach France alive at all. The first time she set out in December 1943, to parachute in, the aircraft had to return because there was fog over the dropping zone. There was fog in Britain that night as well and the plane crashed on landing. Four of the crew were killed and three badly injured but Ann Marie and her colleague, Claude Arnault, escaped with minor injuries.

After a few weeks rest they set off again and parachuted safely into Gascony in south-west France where she became a busy courier to a British Officer, Lieutenant Colonel George Starr, who was one of the outstanding successes of the whole resistance movement. He lived there as a retired mining engineer and once was actually elected Deputy-Mayor of a French town, under the very noses of the Germans, when he was Officer commanding several different Resistance groups.

During her eight months in the field Ann Marie, an ex-WAAF, posed as a local girl, and looked, acted and thought like a local girl—so much so that even when she spoke her native English tongue she had trouble with her grammar. She celebrated her twenty-first birthday in a farmhouse when her colleague, the imperturbable dare-devil Claude, made twenty-one 'candles' for her cake. These were twenty-one pieces of camouflaged fuse, otherwise used for detonating explosives. He was a highly intelligent student and expert saboteur who was at his least concerned when in the greatest danger. Once Ann Marie and he carried four heavy suitcases crammed with explosive and incendiary bombs on public transport and through the streets to a factory in Toulouse that had to be put out of action. He smuggled the bombs into the factory, which manufactured gun-powder, disguised as a workman and later, when the workers had left, placed them in strategic positions amongst the machinery. He expected that the factory would be empty and that the task would take him about twenty minutes. In fact, the Germans placed armed guards to patrol inside the factory that night. He hid amongst the machines and, whilst watching the guards, placed the bombs in position but it took almost an hour and the fuses began to explode prematurely. But even as some of them were exploding he continued to place more and when the place was crowded with alarmed Germans, cut his way through barbed wire around the building and escaped.

Ann Marie wrote a book about her experiences—the only woman agent to write her own—an excellent book with the attractive title of *Moondrop to Gascony*. On page 88 she has this to say about the life of a courier—'When I'm not in Agen, I may be in Condom, in Auch, in Toulouse, in Tarbes or Montregeau. One day I am sent to Auch to collect blank and stamped travel permits. The next I go to Tarbes to take some money to the man who works there. The third I cycle to take a message to the radio operator. Then I am off for three days to Tarbes and Montrejeau where I have to wait for a reply from Jean-Claude or someone else ...'

And at every moment she knew that she might be stopped and searched by German soldiers, police or Gestapo, and she had seen and knew what to expect from them. They had beaten up the children of a couple she knew in front of them, to try and make the parents betray their friends. The children were aged four and two. On that occasion the parents would not talk but, always, there was the possibility that someone would break under torture. There was also the possibility that one of the members of the group was a German spy. The secret agent lived always with those fears. On moonlight nights she waited on the dropping zones for supplies or more agents and when the Germans attacked groups in the area she was in the midst of the battle unpacking and arming grease-covered hand grenades. She slept with a revolver at her bedside, and often cycled through the country roads with a Bren gun hidden in bunches of wild flowers on the carrier. She had hair's breadth escapes also from the dangerous driving of the French Maquis—one day she was in two motor crashes and a motor cycle crash in twenty-four hours.

Her tour of duty finished after eight months with a long dangerous climb over the Pyrenees to Spain.

Nobody would dare to say who was the best of the women agents. Every one of them was what can be best and accurately described as a heroine. Each of them became a heroine when she went into the field because each was intelligent enough to know exactly what she was letting herself in for. Apart from the risk of torture and death at the hands of the savage, ruthless and efficient Gestapo, she accepted also the discomforts and hardships of life in a war-torn country, of primitive conditions, hard work and long hours, without promise of comfort or rest. There is not one instance of one of the girls betraying the trust that was placed in her nor of one shirking her work of responsibility. They were all very different kinds of girls, but each had in common outstanding courage and sense of duty and a superb calmness. They were serene ones who shared also an intense hatred of what German domination meant to conquered nations. And when the conflict ended they returned to the obscurity of their pre-war lives anxious to forget their experiences.

I remember trying to get Christian Granville to talk about her extraordinary experiences as a courier to Lt. Col. Francis Cammaerts, one afternoon in the Polish White Eagle Club in London. She was charming and friendly. She had a paper bag of a very sickly fudge which she liked very much and could not understand why I did not. She would not take 'No' for an answer and pushed the stuff into my mouth saying it was 'beautiful' and would do me good. She had really lost interest in the war but she was a very kind person and for my sake in a desultory fashion spoke modestly and rather disparagingly of her adventures in southern France and north Italy. It was only when she was talking about the lighter moments that her face lit up and her eyes sparkled.

Suzanne Charise. She started her own resistance war when she was 17, subsequently endured betrayal and was then imprisoned. She escaped and reached England 'under fire'.

Odette Churchill, George Cross. She survived a death sentence, torture and a concentration camp. (*Photo: BBC*)

Pearl Witherington. She led an army of the Maquis and fought pitched battles against the Germans.

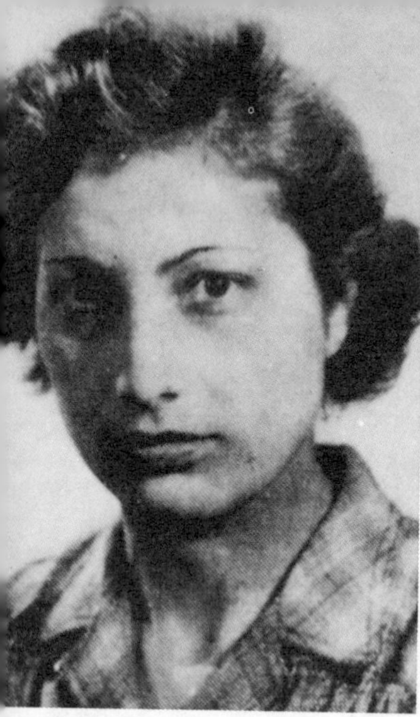

(*above left*) Noor Inayat Khan, George Cross, the gentle heroine they put in chains and executed.

(*above right*) Virginia Hall, 'Marie of Lyons', the American genius with the wooden leg.

(*right*) Yvonne Baseden. She survived capture, torture, Ravensbruck and returned to duty.

(These and all subsequent photos HMSO, Crown Copyright reserved)

This daylight drop of arms, ammunition and supplies took place at Corrèze in August 1944.

Supplies being dropped to the gallant, doomed garrison on the Vercors plateau.

Another successful operation.

Plastic explosive at strategic railway points—like this—wrecked transport arrangements and stopped the movement of troops and supplies.

Paris is in French hands again and the invaders surrender to the Resistance. Place de l'Opéra, August 1944.

to change sides.

She was one of the few survivors of the tragic epic of the Vercors plateau. A desperate pitched battle was fought on the table-land when eleven thousand crack German troops supported by artillery, dive-bombers and paratroopers surrounded and attacked four thousand ill-armed men of the Maquis. The result was inevitable, the French fought until their ammunition was exhausted and the Germans brutally massacred the remnants and the wounded.

Christine was subsequently sent through the German lines to north Italy to report German troop movements and to mix amongst the Polish and Russian troops supporting the Germans, to persuade them to change sides. She was a first-class recruiting officer and helped by her fluency in several languages persuaded hundreds of them to join the resistance. But whilst there a messenger arrived with the grave news that the Commander, Francis Cammaerts, and two other officers had been captured by the Gestapo and were to be executed. This was shattering news which could wreck Allied plans for the landing due to take place very soon on the Mediterranean coast of France. Francis was the 'key-man' of the region—without him everything would be chaotic. Christine took over command; she considered and rejected plans for an armed attempt to rescue the prisoners. The German garrison of the town of Digne, where the prison was situated, was too strong for the recently-mangled Maquis forces. Only some well-thought-out ruse could work. She sent a radio message to Allied Headquarters in North Africa telling them what had happened and asking them to stand by for further messages. Then she dressed in peasant woman clothes and hurried to the town. Looking woebegone and miserable she walked around the prison walls asking gendarmes if she could see 'her husband' Monsieur Cammaerts. One kindly policeman advised her to go to the Police Headquarters and see the Inspector, which she did. On being admitted to his presence she decided to 'put all her cards on the table'. She told him that the Germans were about to execute three high-ranking Allied Officers and that it would not be very long before the victorious Allies would be in charge of the area. They would deal stringently with anyone who had anything to do with the executions; she, herself, was a niece of General Montgomery and would personally see that retribution was meted out and that, generally speaking, it would be in his own interest to help. Whether he believed her, or not, he saw the opportunity of making some profit out of the affair and he told her that it might be possible to bribe a Gestapo officer but that it would cost two million francs —then worth ten thousand pounds. Christine left and radioed headquarters asking for the money to be dropped. The importance headquarters attached to Francis and Christine may be judged from the fact that every stop was pulled out and in a matter of hours a container with the two million francs was dropped and picked up by Christine. The Police Inspector took her to see the Gestapo officer the next morning—the executions were due at dawn the following day. She repeated to the Gestapo man what she had already told the policeman and showed him the money. Indeed, she convinced him and promised him safe conduct and protection if he came with them after releasing the three prisoners. Early next morning, in uniform, he went to the prison where his authority was unchallenged. He went to the cell where Francis and his companions were preparing themselves for death, and pointing his revolver at them ordered them to march. They marched out thinking they were going to the place of execution. But outside the prison the Gestapo officer put his revolver away and told them to follow him and he took them to where Christine was waiting in a car. They all escaped safely.

Shortly afterwards the Americans arrived in the area and she returned to London.

For her outstanding services this magnificent, kindly and beautiful woman was awarded the George Medal, The Order of the British Empire, and the French Croix de Guerre. She died in London in June 1952.

10

THE PRINCESS, GEORGE CROSS

In 1914 a little Indian Princess was born in the Kremlin in Moscow and called Noor Inayat Khan. Her father was an Indian mystic who was on a visit to the Empress of Russia who was deeply interested in mysticism, her mother Ora Baker was a niece of Mary Baker Eddy, the founder of the Christian Science movement. The little Princess grew up to be a slim, sensitive, graceful young lady who charmed everybody she met, and wrote poetry and fairy stories, some of which were used for the children's hour on radio. She spoke several languages because she lived in many countries with her family. They had to leave Germany when Hitler reached power because the Fuhrer had no time for the mild philosophy of the Sufi sect of which Noor's father was the leader. Strangely, years later Hitler's henchmen reserved for the gentle Noor a more inhuman and savage imprisonment than for any of the other women agents.

The family went to live in Paris, where they had made many friends, but moved to England in 1940. Noor, and her brother, joined the RAF. She became a wireless operator and SOE hearing about her knowledge of languages interviewed her and, after some initial hesitation because of her physique and gentle disposition, accepted her for training. Indeed, some parts of the training appalled Noor but she was very fit and determined and shirked nothing. Her instructors were impressed by her keenness but some of them were not convinced that she should be sent into the field—they thought her too sensitive and easily hurt and she had little sense of security. But she was accepted and on 16th June 1943, Noor, called

'Madeleine' in the field, landed by Lysander near Paris. She landed at a time when the Paris circuit was riddled and racked by arrests, double-agents and treachery. The German security services had succeeded in penetrating the organization but not in destroying it completely. For four months she lived quite fearlessly in this highly dangerous area and through her wireless transmitter sent highly valuable information about conditions in Paris to London. She worked from a flat where, on one occasion, she recruited the help of a German soldier to erect her aerial. She arranged and attended some parachute drops near Paris and late in September was instructed to return to London. But she was so conscientious that she postponed her return until a replacement arrived. In the second week of October she went off the air completely, and London were worried, but she came back on the air again after ten days and it seemed as if everything was all right, but London noticed that there was something not quite right with the messages.

In fact, London was quite right: she had been captured and so had her transmitter set and papers. The Germans now in possession of British codes, schedule times and security checks put their own operator on the set and began sending fake transmissions to London. They fooled SOE for a time by sending some genuine news, and they also asked for money and arms drops and won a certain measure of success.

Before being captured Noor had proved herself efficient, resourceful and quite well-qualified for the job. Her capture was not due to any fault on her part but because she was betrayed by a woman trusted by the Resistance forces. She sold Noor's address for five hundred pounds. The traitor was captured and tried after the war.

The Germans knew that Noor was working in the Paris area because their direction-finding vans had picked up her radio signals but they had never been able to pin-point them accurately. Now by a stroke of ill-fortune she had been delivered into their hands. A German officer entered her flat when she was out and waited. He confronted her when she came back and when she realized who he was she turned into a fighting, biting, kicking fury, using every trick she had learned at the SOE training schools. She was no match for him but by the time he had subdued her he was a mass of bleeding bites and bruises.

They took her for interrogation to the Gestapo Headquarters in the Avenue Foch. No sooner had they locked her in a room than she escaped and made her way to the roof but they cornered her there. Some weeks later she escaped from her room again—this time they re-captured her in the house next door—then they sent her to Germany.

After the war the Germans who interrogated her in Paris were questioned and on oath they testified that 'she behaved most bravely after her arrest and we got absolutely no new information out of her at all.' She refused to give the Germans her parole. She was sent to prison at Pforzheim in Germany where by command of high authority she was kept in solitary confinement, fettered by chains to her hands and feet. Even the governor of the prison was horrified by these orders and, on his own account, ordered that her hands should be freed when she was eating!

In September 1944 she and three other girl agents were taken to Dachau concentration camp. The morning after their arrival they were led to a yard and told to kneel by a wall—then holding hands in pairs they were shot through the backs of their necks. The other girls were Yolande Beekman, Elaine Plewman and Madeleine Damerment.

Madeleine Damerment was a very lovely woman of twenty-six when she parachuted to France. As she landed she was seized by German soldiers, interrogated and after imprisonment sent to her fate at Dachau. She escaped from them three years before. She was a reserved, delightful girl with deep religious convictions whose father was the Postmaster General of Lille, a city in northern France. In 1940 her family and herself had become deeply involved with the Resistance in arranging the escape of Allied prisoners of war and passing them safely through escape routes for repatriation to England. She was personally involved in the escape of seventy-five officers and men before the Gestapo got on her track and she had to make her escape to Spain. She had worked then with one of the toughest and most successful heroes of the Resistance, half-English half-French Michael Trotobas. He was captured but escaped; the second time they tried to arrest him he resisted and shot some members of a German raiding party but he was fatally wounded.

She was seized by the Spanish authorities and sent to the notorious Miranda camps where, through ill-treatment and lack of food and neglect she became ill and was released. The British authorities rescued her and arranged her transport to England early in 1941.

After some weeks in hospital Madeleine recuperated at a convent in Hitchin, Hertfordshire and while there volunteered for SOE and return to France. After going through the rigours of training she was parachuted with two men agents on the night of 29th February 1943. They were all captured. It is impossible to imagine her terrible mental anguish when she fell into the hands of the Germans on arrival. She must have realized with horror that SOE itself had been deceived and, perhaps, infiltrated. She was not physically ill-treated on capture but she was subject to the hilarious buffoonery, scoffs and jibes of her captors.

The man who had engineered the deplorable incident was an NCO named Henri Bleicher in the German security forces. He was shrewd, devious and quite unprincipled. Posing as an anti-Nazi he had deceived genuine French patriots and then, unconcernedly, arrested them and when he had finished with them handed them over for transit to Germany, torture and death. By capturing sets and codes and through interrogations of prisoners he had gathered enough information to send fake messages which fooled London for a time. He worked well for his masters and more than 'did his bit' to maintain the reign of terror whilst it lasted. Madeleine was lodged in the Gestapo Headquarters at No. 82 Avenue Foch in Paris until May 1944 and then in prison in Germany, until she was shot in September 1944. Her parents had also been arrested, her mother survived the war in prison in France, her father was hanged in the same camp where Madeleine died.

As late as 1950 the truth of Madeleine's capture had not been revealed as is proven by this letter which her younger sister, Mrs Webb-Damerment wrote to me in that year.

'Dear Mr Gleeson, 6th 5. 1950

'I am French but read with the biggest interest your serial of articles about the F.A.N.Y. My beloved sister Madeleine Damerment was one of them who unfortunately did not come back. I feel it is my duty to write to you about her. Maybe Colonel Buckmaster who told us about her death could tell you better than I will in my bad english—

'Madeleine was born on 11th November 1917 and had always been a very brave girl. In 1940 when the Germans invaded France my father, mother, and Madeleine started to help the French prisoners to escape from the German camps. Then when they could not do anymore they started to work for the resistance in the branch 'Pat O'Leary.' Our work consisted of being there as soon as an english or american plane crashed to give the new civilian clothes and bring them in our home for safety. After a few days the English chief took them to cross France to Portugal and then back to England. For a year we have done all we could (I was young then but still remember). Then one day in May 1941 the Germans came into our house, turned everything upside down and took my father and mother in prison. Madeleine was out at that time. After a few days as they had no prooves (sic) mother and father came back home. But Madeleine started to notice that she was followed all the time. Our chief decided then to send her to England. Unfortunately she was taken in prison in Madrid (Spain) because suspicious. She stayed there forty days under terrible physical torments. Then the British consulate arrived to have her out and she arrived safely in England. Then she went into the FANY and had the same training of which you spoke and then was parachuted early in March 1944. Lived also with the Maquis and completed her mission successfully. Unfortunately she was caught, put in prison in Fresnes near Paris and as she would not speak, was deported in (Excuse me I can't write it properly) She was put then in a cell with a German woman who told us later about her courage in every way. The morning of 13th September 1944 she was taken by the German with another two girls of the F.A.N.Y. and shot through the back and the head.

'This is the terrible ending of the life of a lovely girl. I must tell you also that in March 1944 my parents were taken again in prison. This time the Germans caught them with a English soldier Allen Ratcliffe who was deported with my father. After terrible tortures they both did not come back. My widow mother still live in France and I send her your articles which she is so pleased to have.

'Hoping that I did not take too much of your time, I remain

Your sincerely
G A Webb

'P.S. I enclosed a picture of my sister (the last one she had taken before being parachuted) and a stamped enveloped if you will please sent it back later. Thank you.'

Yolande Beekman was thirty-two when she was shot with the other three girls at Dachau. She was born in Paris but had come to live, and go to school, in England and was living in Hampstead near the famous Heath when war broke out and from there joined the Women's Auxiliary Air Force—the WAAFs. It was not long before her bi-lingual accomplishment and her efficiency marked her out as suitable for interviewing by SOE. She immediately volunteered.

She was trained as a wireless operator and on 17th September 1943 was parachuted to the field with her commanding officer, Guy Bieler. Their sector was about the town of St Quentin in north-west France near the Belgian border. Guy was a huge and formidable Canadian as well as being one of the bravest and most resourceful of men. He sustained a very serious injury to his spine when he hit very hard ground on landing. He would not return to England for treatment but was forced to lie up for many weeks and was left with a permanent limp.

The area where this eminently successful pair worked was a very important one to both sides. It contained seven aerodromes for bombers and fighters engaged in attacking England and intercepting Allied air attacks on Germany. In addition St Quentin was the hub of a canal system which enabled the Germans to move arms and supplies throughout France and as far as Italy. So every sabotage exercise was valuable and this pair were tireless in their efforts. Railway lines, bridges, and electrical installations were continually being blown up and in one outstanding operation Guy demolished the canal gates at St Quentin and sank hundreds of barges. This operation completely stopped the supply of midget submarine parts which the Germans were sending to their divers in Italy.

When Yolande was not helping the sabotage or carrying messages she was busy sending and receiving messages. She used an attic in the town as a wireless station and from there regularly operated her set for three nights a week for three months. It may well be, indeed, that she worked it too regularly—operators were advised to change their location as often as possible in order to confuse the German direction finding units. There must have been some compelling reason for Yolande to use this attic all the time and there is little doubt that it led to her eventual arrest.

Direction-finding vans were seen in the vicinity and one day a suspicious-looking stranger was seen in the street where the attic was situated.

The following day Yolande and Guy were seated in a café when the Gestapo rushed in and arrested them. They were lodged in underground cells at the Gestapo headquarters and when Yolande was seen a few days later by a member of the resistance it was clear that she had been badly knocked about. They were taken to Paris later and from there to Germany. In captivity Guy (Gustave) Bieler continued to win the regard of his friends and of his enemies alike. He made such an impression on the Germans that when he was taken out to be executed the SS mounted a guard of honour to escort him as he limped to the place of execution.

Yolande spent two months in Karlsruhe prison before being taken to Dachau to be shot. A happy cheerful girl, she enjoyed a whirlwind romance whilst training in England. She fell in love with and married one of the instructors, Mr Bateman. They enjoyed a very brief married life before she left for the field.

The fourth girl they killed that morning was the brilliant and beautiful daughter of an English father, Mr Browne-Bartroli, and a Spanish mother—Elaine Sophie Plewman then aged twenty-seven. Elaine was born and spent her childhood years in Marseilles but, with her brother, she also spent many years in, and attended school in England. As well as English and French she spoke Spanish and German fluently. After leaving school this accomplished girl worked in an exporting firm in Leicester and met an Englishman, Tom Plewman, to whom she became engaged. Later she went to Madrid where she worked in the British Embassy, and in the Embassy at Lisbon in Portugal. Then she returned to London and worked in the Spanish section of the Ministry of Information. In July 1942 she and Tom Plewman, then an officer in the British Army, were married at a church in Kensington, London.

They enjoyed but a brief married life for he had to return to his regiment. Her brother, Albert, had become a member of SOE and through him Elaine was interviewed by, and became a member of, the Organization.

She parachuted to France on 13th August 1944—to the area about Marseilles where she had been born and brought up. She went there as courier to a gallant and aggressive officer, Major Charles Skepper, who had already put the horrors of one facet of the war behind him. He had fought against the Japanese in the Far East and had been captured and ill-treated in one of the notorious Japanese prisoner-of-war camps. They had exchanged him as being totally disabled but back in London he recovered and volunteered for service with the Resistance. He, and his wireless operator, Arthur Steele, a twenty-year-old music student from London had plenty of work for Elaine. They proved to be a formidable team in an area which contained two hundred and forty thousand German troops, artillery batteries and gun emplacements waiting to repulse the Allied invasion expected from North Africa. To assist this invasion London was thirsty for every scrap of information and Elaine travelled backwards and forwards tirelessly collecting intelligence and passing it to the wireless operator for transmission. She was attending parachute drops as well, and passing messages to and from the various resistance groups, teaching about arms and explosives and taking part in sabotage activities.

Her brother, who sometimes worked in the area, was annoyed one day when he met her in Marseilles carrying a heavy load of explosives which she was going to use on a sabotage mission herself. He took the package and went with her to carry out the operation but he thought that she was being pushed a bit too hard.

The German security services were very much on the alert in that area and very anxious to apprehend the British spies whom they knew to be working there. In the end they were betrayed by a woman member of the group who had a German lover. She told him the address of the flat where Skepper was resting and the Gestapo rushed it and arrested him. They sent him back to their headquarters but some of them remained hidden in the flat to await more arrivals. Later that afternoon Elaine and Arthur Steele heard about the raid and were under the impression that the Germans still held their officer in the flat. They determined to try and rescue him. When they reached the flat they saw two Germans outside and drawing their pistols approached them but as they did so the other Germans rushed from the house and overpowered them. They were all ill-treated, but refusing to betray others, were sent to Paris and then to Germany where all three were killed.

11

DIANA AND HER FRIENDS

The 'radio game' was one of the most dreadful features of the war waged by the secret forces of both sides. In spite of all the precautions that SOE took mistakes were made. Codes were improved until they became almost unbreakable; each wireless operator was carefully trained in confidential checks known only to themselves and London, and there was also the added security that each operator had a personal style and touch on the key which was believed to be as individual and hard to imitate as fingerprints. Yet the Germans, as we have seen, having captured SOE sets, times of schedules and codes were able to deceive London and arrange fake parachute drops in which they captured agents, arms and large sums of money. Now and then an SOE agent captured by the Germans acquiesced through torture, terror or threats. The Germans also used their own skilled operators to operate sets and imitate the style and touch of a genuine agent. They were sometimes helped by the fact that the listeners in Britain knew that an agent transmitting from the field might be doing so in hard and hazardous conditions and would make allowances for this. Once a captured agent purposely omitted his personal sign from a message he was forced at gun point to send. Sadly, a reply was sent back telling him he had forgotten to include the vital signal and to be more careful in future. The Germans were not pleased with him either!

One of the victims of this evil game was Squadron Leader Diana Hope Rowden, a splendid woman who had joined SOE and was sent into the field by Lysander on 16th June 1943. The daughter of a wealthy British family, her father was

Scottish, she spent her youth pleasantly on the Mediterranean shores of southern France where her father kept a yacht called —very appropriately in Diana's case—*Sans Peur*.

On the outbreak of war her mother returned to England but Diana felt it her duty to assist the war effort and became a nurse caring for wounded British prisoners of war. Inevitably, she became involved in helping them to escape and make their way back to Britain by way of the Pyrenees and Spain. Then when the authorities became suspicious she too had to take the same route. Back in England she joined the WAAFs and served for a time with Air Intelligence in the department of the Chief of Air Staff and later as Intelligence Officer at the Royal Air Force station at Moreton-in-Marsh in the West Country of England.

In 1943 she came to the attention of SOE and when given the opportunity immediately volunteered for work as a secret agent in France. She was sent as a courier to an area in north-east France bordering Switzerland. She jumped with her wireless operator, an admirable, tough young Scot named John Young. There were several groups in that part of France short of communications with London, so the pair were very welcome and immediately very busy, Diana travelling about collecting and delivering messages whilst John stuck at his set sending and receiving. When they were free from these duties they were occupied in parachute drops and arms training but disaster befell when the Germans swooped and captured several members of their group including the leader.

Diana and John escaped and continued on their own working from a remote sawmill near a village called Clairvaux. The work continued to be strenuous and demanding so they were delighted when John received a message saying that an agent had been dropped in another part of France and was on his way to assist them.

Indeed he had been dropped but, through the machinations of the Germans with their radio game, right into the hands of the Gestapo who formed the reception committee. They took the agent to their headquarters and minutely examined all the papers he was carrying—including a personal letter to

John Young from his wife.

It may have been that the genuine agent, shocked and hurt by his immediate arrest through what may have seemed to him to be London's fault, co-operated with his captors; on the other hand they found plenty of information on him that told them that he was on his way to join Diana and John. Anyway, they took his clothes, found one of their own men, dressed him in the agent's clothes, primed him and sent him to the sawmill. When he arrived he was warmly welcomed, he handed over the messages and the letter from John's wife and succeeded in convincing Diana and John and the others at the mill that he was genuine. Then he said that he had left extra luggage in the village and he walked back there with the son of the house. Later that day Diana went to the village where she met him and walked back to the mill with him. They were followed by Germans who threw a cordon around the place and rushed in firing their pistols into the walls and ceilings, and arrested John and Diana, and the false agent. That night the false agent returned to the mill in his true colours and producing his pistol demanded that John's wireless transmitting set be handed over but the women who were there bravely denied all knowledge of it and the Germans never found it.

John and Diana were taken to the Gestapo headquarters in Paris for interrogations but the Germans could get nothing useful out of them. They were both sent to Germany, John was executed in September 1944 and Diana at the extermination camp at Natzweiler on 6th July of the same year. She and two other women agents were killed by injections of poison—phenol—and immediately their bodies were thrown into the crematorium ovens. The other girls were Andrée Borrel and Vera Leigh. Diana, who had somehow managed to get a piece of tartan ribbon, wore it in her hair when they killed her.

Andrée Borrel was brought up by her widowed mother in Lille, where she was born in 1919. Life was not easy for her mother and when they moved to Boulogne-sur-Seine Andrée got a job as a shop girl to help the family budget. When war started she became a nurse and also an enthusiastic member of the Resistance. She was a tough, intelligent girl with a love for adventure, a preference for sweaters and slacks and enjoyed nothing better than a good sabotage operation like blowing up an important railway bridge or some German officers' cars. She was gifted also with a quick intelligence and was trusted implicitly by SOE on delicate and important missions.

After working for two years with a Resistance group in the south of France she was forced to escape over the Pyrenees when her group was shattered by the Germans. In England her personality, experience and determination made her a perfect recruit for SOE and she became a keen and brilliant pupil. With Lise de Baissac, the talented, demure 'widow', she was parachuted to France on 24th September 1942—the first two girls to arrive in this fashion and their reception was arranged by another of the 'girls' Yvonne Rudelatt, the grandmother.

Andrée made her way to Paris to prepare the way for her chief, Major Francis Suttill, who subsequently built one of the largest Resistance networks in France. Posing as his sister she accompanied him on reconnaissance missions over vast areas of the country. He was supposed to be a commercial traveller in agricultural machinery but Andrée did most of the talking because she was better at selling and also because his French accent was very bad.

In Paris the position was tense and dangerous. The Germans had succeeded in penetrating a good section of the Resistance and there were many and continuing arrests. Andrée, a quite fearless woman, continued to carry out her courier business and sabotage with a sublime indifference. For nine months she worked ceaselessly and well and earned the highest commendations from her superiors.

The blow fell on 24th June 1943 when the Gestapo learned the address of the Chief and arrested him. They went to Andrée's house as well and arrested her in bed. After the usual interrogations she was sent to Karlsruhe in Germany and from there to Natzweiler for poison injections.

Courage is classless—these girls came from all walks of life—shopgirls, nurses, one was a countess, another a princess. Vera Leigh was the daughter of a wealthy industrialist who was herself the part-owner of a famous Paris fashion house. Vera was born in Leeds, the daughter of an American industrialist who was also a well-known racehorse owner and trainer with stables in England and France. One of his best-known horses was Epinard, winner of several French classic races in the 1920s and also of the British Stewards' Cup. Epinard also sired several good horses.

Vera became an excellent horsewoman, was a member of a famous hunt and an accomplished point-to-point rider. When she was twenty-three she became a director of the well-known fashion house, Reboux, in Paris and later of 'La Grande Maison Valois' which was patronized by ladies of high fashion from all over the world.

She remained in Paris for a time after it was occupied by the Germans. Her father's American citizenship enabled her to claim neutrality, but she became involved in the Resistance and went to Lyons where she met the redoubtable Virginia Hall and through her became very active in the Pat O'Leary escape route for allied servicemen. Like several of her colleagues she had eventually to use the escape line herself and in Spain she was arrested and interned for a time in the concentration camp, Miranda.

When she was released she continued her journey to London arriving at Christmas 1942. It was not long before SOE became interested and Vera was only too anxious to return to continue her work against the Germans. She was forty when she began her rigorous training but she was very fit; indeed, her instructors reported that she more than kept up with the men who were training with her and that she was the best shot of them all.

She arrived near Paris by Lysander on 14th June 1943 and went straight to Paris to begin her duties as courier. She arrived at a time when the resistance in Paris was riddled with treachery. The German NCO counter espionage agent, Bleicher, had infiltrated his men into the group and even he, himself, was in touch with Vera's chief who was a courageous and patriotic Frenchman but he had been hoodwinked by the NCO's pose as an anti-Nazi. Vera well knew the risks she ran by returning to Paris, she was known to many people and she could not know in which direction their sympathies lay. She made no attempt to disguise herself, she remained the well-groomed, fashionable, well-to-do Parisienne of old. In spite of the wartime shortages and restrictions the ladies of Paris kept up their traditional couture to as high a standard as was possible.

One day she was seen by her brother-in-law; she saw him too and tried to avoid him and when he confronted her tried to make out she was someone else. But he was not deceived and she relented and embraced him. Luckily, he too was in the resistance running an escape route and she helped him with his escapes as well as continuing with her courier duties. A few days after she arrived there was a fresh crop of arrests, Andrée Borrel was one of those captured.

She changed her residence frequently and acted with discretion but such precautions were useless against treachery and her activities were reported to Bleicher, the German NCO. He had her shadowed, allowing her to remain at liberty in the hope that she would lead him to her colleagues. But Vera was too discreet to do this and eventually he gave orders for her arrest.

She was picked up by the Gestapo in the Café Mas in the Place des Ternes in Paris on 30th November 1943. She had been at liberty for just over five months during which time she had carried out her duties extremely efficiently, bravely and successfully.

After imprisonment in Paris and Karlsruhe in Germany she was taken to Natzweiler and killed by poison with Diana Rowden and Andrée Borrel. Just before the three girls were executed they were seen by two other prisoners at Natzweiler who survived and gave evidence at the War Trials after the end of hostilities—Lt.-Commander Pat O'Leary and a member of the Belgian resistance Dr Boogaerts. Dr Boogaerts threw Andrée Borrel some cigarettes and she threw him back her money bag which contained her tobacco pouch. He brought these articles back with him and passed them over to her sister.

At the War Trials it was stated, 'The party arrived at Natzweiler at about three o'clock in the afternoon on 6th July 1944. They were seen by a number of other prisoners; it was somehow learnt that they were British and French. Lt.-Commander O'Leary and the Belgian, Dr Boogaerts, succeeded in making brief contact with two of the girls whose cells faced the infirmary. As the afternoon wore on it became apparent that some unusually sinister business was afoot. The authorities ordered all prisoners to be in their huts by 8 p.m., to put up the black-out and not show their faces at any window. Between 9.30 and 10.30 p.m. the girls were taken singly from the bunker to the crematorium. There they were injected and immediately cremated. The pleas that all concerned were only anxious to act as humanely as possible collapse in view of the fact that nobody took any steps to safeguard the legal rights of the prisoners and that the doctor did not consider it necessary to ascertain what drug he was injecting.

'There was no evidence to disbelieve the evidence of Bruttel, the medical orderly of the camp, given in his affidavit and in evidence that the only substance which he took with him to the crematorium, in obedience to Dr Plaza, the camp medical officer, was phenol.' The Camp doctor was convicted and hanged.

Lt.-Colonel Francis Cammaerts, you will remember, was in charge of Resistance forces of an extensive and extremely important area in the south and south-east of France. He escaped death by inches on several occasions and once thought he was being led to stand in front of the firing squad when, in fact, he was being rescued by the brilliant strategy of the Polish Countess, Christine Granville. On a previous occasion he narrowly escaped as well when the Germans infuriated by the consistent and successful sabotage operations he was organizing mounted a vast security operation in the area where they knew him to be. He was never quiescent—when he had enough arms and explosives he was blowing up railway lines and bridges and electrical installations; when he ran out of explosives he taught his groups how to sabotage by putting sand in the oil boxes of locomotives, removing vital parts from engines and changing destination labels on trains so that they went everywhere except the right place. The Germans, as they say, were livid, and they swooped on him and his courier who was, at that time, a forty-two-year old Irish woman, Cecily Lefort.

She had been thoroughly and happily involved in all the sabotage that was going on and was proving herself a fit and capable assistant to the irrepressible Francis but, fatally for her, she once neglected his advice and visited the house of a friend who was, she knew, suspected by the Germans. Whilst she was there two car-loads of Gestapo men arrived, surrounded the house and captured her. Francis was away on a mission at the time.

A messenger brought him the bad news and he at once risked life and limb by returning to the village where the Germans were waiting for him to see if he could mount a rescue operation for Cecily. But he learned that she had been immediately removed to the prison at Lyon where many thousands of German troops were situated. He had to disperse the group for the time being and lie low—but not for long. Soon he was busy again taking toll for what they did to Cecily.

At Lyon they subjected her to long and brutal interrogations because their patience had become exhausted and they were anxious to crush the saboteurs—they wanted to know the names of the group and the location of the leader, but they were wasting their time on Cecily. She revealed nothing.

She had landed by Lysander in France on 16th June 1943 and had been captured on 10th September the same year. Cecily, who was known as a capable yachtswoman in happier times, had married a Frenchman and lived with him in France for several years. In 1940 when the Germans approached Paris she left for England and through friends got in touch with SOE. When she landed in France in June she was accompanied by two other women who paid the supreme sacrifice—

Diana Rowden and Noor Inyata Khan.

There are no precise details of Cecily's fate. It is known for certain that they sent her eventually to Ravensbruck, the dreadful camp where thousands of unfortunate women were done to death and that her health broke down there early in 1945. She was either worked to death, as was customary, or died in the gas chambers, which they used to accelerate the death rate. Like Yvonne Rudellat who died in similar circumstances in the other hell camp, Belsen, she died shortly before the collapse of Germany.

Vera Atkins, who made it her business to find out the fate of the girls had this to say of her charges. (It is interesting to know that after Vera had questioned Bleicher, the German NCO, who survived the war he said about her, 'I was startled one morning to be visited by a very pretty young woman officer in uniform. She turned out to have more aplomb than all the other officers put together. She boxed me in with astonishing ease and consummate tactics ...')

'In April 1945 prisoners began to return from Germany, and among them a few survivors from concentration camps. Some of our officers brought back news of others who had been killed. Of the women, Odette was the first to return. Next came Yvonne and then Eileen Nearne. All these at some stage had passed through the huge and notorious women's camp at Ravensbruck, and all these, at some stage, had seen some of our missing girls.

'By the autumn of 1945, we abandoned hope for the men and women who had not returned. Already there was a special mission at work in Germany combing through official papers and prison records for the names of our people, but the result was discouraging. Only two of them were traced.

'After winding up the London office in December 1945, I went to Germany to try and find out the fate of our friends, through the interrogation of war criminals, and by carrying out investigations on the spot. It was a case of following every clue and piecing together bits of evidence.

'Then started the hunt for those German Gestapo and concentration camp officials who alone knew the final truth.

Some were already in one or other of the numerous internment camps spread about the four zones of Germany. Others were still at large. It was a slow job, but in the end I had all the answers except for a very small number where it would have been necessary to pursue enquiries into the Russian zone, to which we had no access.

'There were dramatic moments, face to face with some German brute in a pretty close battle of wits. I was greatly helped by the thorough knowledge I had by this time acquired of the set-up within the Gestapo and the various concentration camps. It was possible to play off one man against another, and I was quite determined to get as near the truth as possible.

'These interrogations were horrible and nightmarish beyond belief. How vividly I seemed to feel the presence of those whose fate we were discussing. I am afraid I used to try and make the Germans understand what they had done. A silly effort at reform, but sometimes it broke down the barriers built around a blackened conscience, and they became semi-human. In this mood, they would perhaps describe a scene in detail.

'There is no doubt that the wonderful bearing of our men and women made a deep impression on all who came into contact with them. They seemed to have a faith and pride of purpose which carried them through the darkest hours. It was finally proved that Diana Rowden, Denise Borell and Vera Leigh were given injections and cremated at Natzweiler. Eileen Plowman, Noor Inyata Khan, Yvonne Beekman and Madeleine Damerment were taken to Dachau and killed by revolver shots. Lilian Rolfe, Denise Bloch and Violette Szabo were killed by shooting at Ravensbruck. Yvonne Ruddelat died of exhaustion at Belsen.'

12

ODETTE, GEORGE CROSS

The very first young woman to go to France for SOE was a very beautiful young Parisian actress named Giliana Balmaceda Gerson. Her husband Victor Gerson was a member of SOE who founded and maintained an enormous escape line which stretched from Holland and Belgium right across France to Spain. Through it several thousands of escaped prisoners of war, refugees from Hitler, hunted Jews and other enemies of the Reich were conveyed to freedom. It was called the 'Vic line' after its founder. He and a group, exclusively Jews, except for the wireless operator, looked after and shepherded the escapees.

In May 1941 he wanted to find out as much as he could about conditions in France and to sound out some contacts. His wife volunteered to go. She had been born in Chile and using her neutral passport she made her way openly to southern France and spent six weeks collecting every scrap of information she could and alerting sympathizers. She returned, again quite openly, through Spain and Gibraltar.

Another wife Adele le Chene, the oldest woman agent of them all, went to the field with her husband. He was a fifty-year-old London hotel manager who ran a small group in the south of France. Adele, then forty-eight, arrived by felucca with Odette Churchill on 31st October 1942. Talking about it after to Elizabeth Nicholas, who wrote *Death be not Proud*, her husband said with a grin, 'I went into the racket to get away from my wife but she followed me in.'

She worked as courier to her husband for a year performing very valuable work and tackling any task that arose efficiently and cheerfully. Her husband was captured eventually but was lucky enough to survive and she returned to England in August 1943.

Another husband and wife team who shared a perilous period together in Paris when treachery and double-dealing were at their height were Jack and Francine Agazarian. She joined her husband there on 17th March 1943, having arrived by Lysander and lived and worked with him until June of that year when they were both forced to flee back to Britain as the circuit was being cruelly and systematically penetrated and wrecked by counter German intelligence and traitors.

They were very nearly captured on one ocasion through an off-shoot of the infamous German *coup* 'North Pole' by which several Allied agents were captured in Holland. Two false agents were sent by the Germans to Paris to contact and betray a member of the Resistance there. When the fake agents approached a member of the Paris circuit he, very carelessly and without checking, told them to go to a café where they would find members of the Resistance. They went to the café—near the Sacré Coeur in Montmartre—and found the Agazarians, Andrée Borrel and a French couple deeply engrossed in a game of poker! The fake agents were accepted as genuine and as a result learned much which led to further arrests. The Agazarians were ordered to return to England—subsequently Jack, a truly heroic figure, went back to the field and was captured, imprisoned, refused to talk and was shot six weeks before the end of the war in Flossenberg in Germany.

At the same time in Paris Madame Julienne Besner was also working with her husband. They lived in a flat which was used as a safe house and she also acted as courier. She was, in fact, courier to one of the most controversial characters of the Resistance—a colourful and daring ex-pilot named Henri Dericourt who was the centre of a sensational treason trial in Paris after the war.

He did an enormous amount of useful work for the Resistance but—at the same time—it was alleged by some that he was working for the Germans. He was acquitted at the trial when a number of genuine patriots and honest men were shown to be deeply divided in their convictions about him.

Julienne, who worked for the Resistance in France before training with SOE, worked in the turbulent Paris area from May 1943 until April 1944.

It was generally acknowledged that Lt.-Col. George Starr who ran an outstanding circuit was extremely lucky in his wireless operator, Yvonne Cormeau who was a WAAF before joining SOE. George Starr was the leader whom the people of Castelnau-sur-l'Auvignon elected deputy-Mayor.

Yvonne proved to be superb at her job. For thirteen months after she was parachuted in on 23rd August 1943, she regularly and accurately tapped out messages which kept her vitally important circuit in constant touch with London. She sent four hundred different messages in one year, which must have been the record; she became so busy, indeed, that she was given an assistant.

'I transmitted from the same house for two months and the German direction finders knew all about it and that it was a woman—they could tell this by the touch. On three occasions I was betrayed, once by a Spanish communist but they never found me,' Yvonne told me. For these two months she was transmitting from a remote hamlet where there was not even running water. From the house she was using she could see all around for three miles. 'Another thing that confused the Germans was that there were eight Castlenaus in all and they never knew from which one I was transmitting,' she said.

Yvonne, who was trained with Noor Inyata Khan and Yolande Beekman, did her magnificent job and survived safely.

One resourceful young woman, Blanche Charlet, was captured, interrogated and imprisoned by the Germans. After eleven months in French gaols she managed to escape, join an escape route and make her way back to England by Royal Naval launch. She arrived on the southern coast of France by felucca from Gibraltar on 1st September 1942.

She joined a young fashion designer who had been trained as a wireless operator in England—he worked for Vogue. Acting as his courier Blanche found him safe houses and distributed his messages to the various leaders and resistance groups over a wide area. One day, however, he was engaged in sending a very long message and the direction finders had time to get an accurate fix on his location. They found him at his set. A few minutes afterwards Blanche arrived at the house with some messages for him and she too was captured.

Mrs Sansom had put her three young daughters in bed when she sat down in her home in a Somerset village early in 1942 and switched on the radio to listen to the BBC news. It was all about the war which seemed so far away—North Africa, Greece, Russia and about air raids, marshalling yards and food rationing. It seemed to be the same kind of thing every night and though she knew that it was vitally important to thousands of homes from which the men-folk were absent and probably involved, it had no great impact in her kitchen.

Then, after the news, a pleasant voice in an interesting way talked about photographs and the war effort and Mrs Sansom became more interested when the speaker talked about pictures taken in France. Thousands of people had taken snap-shots on the beaches of France, and in the countryside. She remembered that she had; and said the voice, these were now lying in drawers and in photograph albums all over the British Isles. But, said the voice, these were needed now by the Admiralty because they might be of great use in the planning of future attacks on the continent—perhaps, even in the event of invasion. The speaker finished by appealing to his listeners to turn out these snap-shots and send them to the Admiralty in London with, if possible, a description of where they were taken, and any other details the listener could add to identify the location.

So Mrs Sansom turned out her snap-shots, put them in an envelope and described exactly where they were taken. She added that she knew the area very well because she was French and had been brought up there. Then she addressed the envelope and made the error which was to lead to her remarkable, sometimes dreadful, but always magnificent series of adventures. Odette addressed it to the War Office in London, instead of to the Admiralty. And in the War Office somebody who opened the envelope and knew nothing about the Admiralty appeal sent it to what, he thought, would be the most interested department—Special Operations Executive, the 'Firm'.

Captain Jepson, SOE's most experienced recruiting officer, was interested and consequently Odette was very surprised to receive a rather noncommital acknowledgement which invited her to come and see the writer.

She became even more puzzled during the subsequent interview because the Captain mentioned that there was work which she might well do for the department. She said she would be happy to help but that it would have to be part-time because she had her three small daughters to look after! She became a little scandalized when he suggested that, perhaps, somebody else could look after the children. And she really did not know what to think when he said that she might return to France to help them there—'I don't think I am the right person and I *do* have my three children to care for,' she repeated almost angrily. But he continued speaking about the work, about its importance to the Allied effort and about the kind of people who were needed and how important such people could be. He begged her not to turn it down right away but to go away and think about it. When Captain Jepson found somebody whom he judged to be suitable he did not easily give up.

Odette went back to the Somerset village and thought hard about it. She knew France well and was an expert bi-linguist. She had been born Odette Marie Celine Brailly on 28th April 1912 in Amiens. Her father had been killed fighting the Germans in the First World War. She had serious illnesses as a child, when she was eight she went blind and when she recovered from that caught rheumatic fever and spent many months in bed. Her mother moved to Normandy, near Dieppe, which she judged to be healthier and Odette thrived in the sea air. In 1930 she married an Englishman, Roy Sansom and in 1932 she moved to England.

After considering Captain Jepson's proposal for a week she

phoned him up—'I am prepared to join for training and if I am then considered suitable I will go to France,' she said. She had found a convent in Brentwood, in Essex, which would accept and care for the three little daughters. Her training satisfactorily concluded, SOE decided that she should go not as a courier, nor a wireless operator, but simply as a lone executive organizer to the town of Auxerre to establish herself there, explore the possibilities of recruiting others and have a safe house to where new agents who were arriving in France could be sent. Similar instructions were given, you will remember, to Lise de Baissac, the demure 'widow'. Odette too became a 'widow' named Odette Metayer whose husband had died of bronchitis and she had come to live quietly in the country to be away from the rude and boisterous soldiery.

Getting Odette into the field turned out to be a major task. She was to leave by Whitley bomber which would take her to Gibraltar from where she would continue her journey by felucca to the Mediterranean coast of France. As the bomber taxied out to take off, another aircraft came in to land and they hit each other, Odette was unharmed. A week afterwards she was waiting in a Lysander to take off for a landing strip in France when a messenger ran out to stop them—the reception committee in France had been discovered and arrested by the Germans. A week afterwards she sat waiting for take-off in a flying boat at Plymouth, bound for Gibraltar, when a storm blew up and the trip was cancelled. A week afterwards she took off in a Whitley bomber which remained air-borne for only a few minutes and crashed a few feet from a cliff edge—she was unharmed. So she was sent to join a troopship in Scotland which eventually landed her safely at Gibraltar. From Gibraltar she sailed with six other agents including two women agents—Marie Theresa Le Chene who was forty-eight and Mary Herbert, the agent who married her officer, Claude de Baissac, in the field—and after an eight-day voyage arrived in France near Cannes. Her instructions were to report to an agent named Raoul who would arrange her journey to Auxerre. He was Captain Peter Churchill who was then on his third mission to France. A shrewd, fearless and brilliant organizer, he had won great distinction by his invaluable work in the field and was one of the first of the great architects who laid the foundations for the success of the Resistance movement. He was in charge of a large and busy sector and when Odette arrived was woefully short of capable assistants. He was too busy to arrange for her journey to Auxerre just then, he asked her if she would help during her temporary stay in his area. She agreed and carried out several jobs for him with such efficiency and dispatch that he asked her if she would remain permanently. She agreed and so did London, after some initial hesitation.

They were very nearly captured soon afterwards. Peter was ordered to return to London for a conference and a Lysander was sent to pick him up. Odette and two others, including their wireless operator, Lieutenant Alec Rabinovitch, a Jew, waited on the landing strip and heard the Lysander approaching. Peter was just about to flash the recognition signals when a searchlight was switched on from the ground. The strip was surrounded by German soldiers who had heard about the operation through a traitor and hoped to make an important 'killing'. Peter and his companions broke up and dived into the shrubland, the Lysander circled once more and not getting the agreed signal lights, swooped away back to England. As Odette ran through the darkness she heard the whimperings of dogs which were following her tracks. Luckily, she was running towards a river. With a feeling of great relief she waded into the icy-cold water, crossed to the far bank, and got away. They all escaped.

The traitor had given everything away and in the days that followed several members of the group were arrested and imprisoned. Peter, Odette and Alec had to leave immediately and set up their headquarters elsewhere. They chose the village of St Joritz in the Haute Savoie, near the borders of Switzerland, about twenty-five miles from Geneva. They quickly re-established themselves and soon St Joritz was the hub of a very active sector and an important communications centre for the whole of France. Alec was a first-class operator and he found an ideal location in the mountains from which his signals were heard loud, clear and frequently in Britain. Peter made his journey to London for the conference by the same Lysander that brought Francis Cammaerts into the field, and whilst he was away Odette carried on successfully as the officer in charge.

In St Joritz, they used the local hotel, called the Hôtel de la Poste as their headquarters. It was managed by Jean and Simone Collet who were trusted friends of the Resistance movement. One afternoon Odette was having lunch in the dining room when a stranger entered and introduced himself to her—he was Sergeant Henri Bleicher of the German security services. Treachery had continued and he knew all about St Joritz and its active group. Instead of swooping straightaway he had decided to try and infiltrate the group himself so that he might spread his net wider and deeper and catch bigger and more important 'fish'. He told Odette that he was a representative of a very large group of German officers who wished to contact London in order that a *coup* be arranged to oust Hitler, finish the war and make an honourable peace with the Allies. He asked for a transmitting set and codes so that he could contact London direct. Odette told him that that was ridiculous—she had neither—but, she said, it might be possible to arrange for a message giving details of his proposals to be sent. He left her saying that he would contact her again. She wrote a report of the meeting and gave it to Alec who sent it off immediately. London replied quickly telling her to have nothing more to do with Henri, that she was in grave peril, that she should dissolve the circuit at once and disappear. It added that Peter was on his way back.

On 15th April he arrived by parachute. Odette was waiting for him on the field, and he said that they must pack up and leave the district without delay. They were both tired and dawn was not far away so they decided to sleep for a few hours at the Hôtel de la Poste. They had not long to sleep. Odette woke to find the owner knocking at her door—there was a man downstairs who wanted to see her at once. Unsuspectingly she walked down—to Henri Bleicher who was waiting with a pistol in his hand, other men holding pistols stood about. She was marched back upstairs with a pistol in her back, to the room where Peter was sleeping. 'You are under arrest—you are Peter Churchill the British agent and saboteur,' Bleicher told him.

Alec Rabinovitch, the wireless operator, was not captured. He sent news to London about the arrests and how Bleicher had once again shattered a circuit. Alec escaped back to England through Spain and was later parachuted to the field again. Eventually they captured him too and, because he was a Jew, gave him a particularly bad time before killing him.

Peter and Odette were lodged in an Italian prison for three weeks and then taken to Fresnes prison in Paris. From here Odette was taken on several occasions to the Gestapo Headquarters for interrogation and when they could get nothing out of her by questioning they tortured her. They put a red-hot poker on her backbone—but she would not talk, then one of them got a pair of pincers and slowly and very deliberately pulled off all her toe nails. She did not talk—back in her cell she tore up strips of clothing to bandage her feet.

They took her back to the Gestapo Headquarters once again and she hobbled into a room where a group of Officers sat at a table. They spoke in German, reached a decision and then the chairman told her in French, 'You are condemned to die on two counts. The first is because you are a British spy and the second because you are a Frenchwoman'.

She was the only one of the women agents who was formally sentenced to death, yet she was one of the three who survived—the other two were Yvonne Baseden and Eileen Nearne. This sentence was, of course, a refinement of torture because whilst she was a prisoner she never knew at what time of the day or night they might carry out the execution—every time the door of her cell was opened it might be the executioner who stood there. But, as time went on, that was almost the least of her worries. Shortly after her sentence she sent for the Commandant of Fresnes and told him that she was, in fact Mrs Churchill, the wife of Peter. The Germans believed him to be closely related to the Prime Minister, Winston Churchill.

Bleicher never gave up. After she had been tortured and

sentenced to death, he came to see her in Fresnes to try to recruit her to his nefarious designs and, like the devil who tempted Christ, he promised her the best of the world's pleasures but, like the devil, he was sent off with a flea in his ear.

She was kept in France for a year and then sent to Germany. On the railway journey she met six other women agents who had been captured and were going to their deaths —Andrée Borrel, Vera Leigh, Diana Rowden, Yolande Beekman, Madeleine Damerment and Elaine Plewman. She was handcuffed to Yolande. At Karlsruhe prison in Germany she was separated from the others, locked in a cell for eight weeks, and then sent to the terrible Ravensbruck concentration camp for women. On the way she suffered one more blow—literally as well as metaphorically—A man called her name out and she went and stood before him. He gave her a smashing blow in the mouth with his clenched fist—'I give you that for Winston Churchill—with my compliments,' he said as she fell.

In Ravensbruck they put her in an underground cell (in the Bunker, which was the camp prison) in solitary confinement in darkness for three months. Three times a day—not that she knew night from day—the jailer switched on the bright lights which blinded her as he handed in her meagre ration, first a mug of watery ersatz coffee and a slice of black bread; later a bowl of thin soup made from unwashed scraps of vegetables and later another mug of coffee.

When the British invasion forces landed on the south coast of France they punished her—they turned the heat up and up in her cell until it became a raging inferno and they cut off her food for a week. 'You have been punished by the order of the Gestapo,' the Camp Commandant, Fritz Suhren, told her.

But they nearly killed her and that, apparently, was not their intention. She became so ill that they moved her to an upstairs cell exactly opposite the entrance to their busy crematorium.

In April 1945 an order was sent by Himmler, the head of the Gestapo, that all the prisoners in the Bunker were to be executed, but Suhren, for reasons of his own, chose to keep seven of them alive.

On 29th April 1945 she was thirty-three. On 3rd May an SS man came to her cell and called her out telling her to leave her belongings—'This is the end,' she thought. He led her to a car where Suhren was seated and she was told to sit beside him. 'I am taking you to the Americans,' he said and drove until they reached the first of the American troops.

Suhren stopped and said to an American officer, 'This is Frau Churchill. She has been a prisoner. She is a relation of Winston Churchill, the Prime Minister of England.' And Odette added, 'And this is Fritz Suhren, Commandant of Ravensbruck Concentration Camp. Please make him your prisoner.' To Suhren she said, 'Give me your revolver,' and she took it and walked away.

13

SUZANNE AND BLANCHE

Suzanne Charisse was one of the last of the girls to be trained by SOE and she hardly needed training because she had already been active with the Resistance forces for four years. Then when through imprisonment and hardship she had nearly reached the end of her resources she had been rescued by the Royal Navy and brought to England in April 1944. After she had recovered her health and strength she volunteered to return to the field and was still training when France was liberated by the Allies.

In fact as a slim young blonde of seventeen she had started her own resistance groups with youngsters of her own age and assisted by her three elderly aunts. They, and her father, who had been a soldier, had seen the German armies in action in the 1914-18 war, just as their parents before them had suffered under the similar armies in the Franco-Prussian war of 1870. The family lived in Le Havre not far from the traditional battle grounds. Suzanne grew up there and learned neither to be surprised not intimidated by anything the Germans might do. It was just as well she had, and lucky also that she was blessed with the personality and character that heroines are made of because she was to meet them—and their lackeys—at their worst.

When the victorious German armies of 1940 approached Le Havre she was forced to join the ranks of fleeing refugees who, taking what they could hold, streamed through the roads and were barbarously machine-gunned and bombed by German pilots who held then the undisputed mastery of the French skies. The advancing Germans passed her at a village near

Caen where she found shelter. They also left many hidden pockets of French troops behind them in the depths of the countryside. Many of these soldiers threw their rifles away in the hope that if they were captured they would be treated as civilians and not held in prisoner-of-war camps. Suzanne rounded up her friends and collected and hid the rifles for the times when they would be wanted again—it never occurred to her that the pathetic retreat she was witnessing was the end of the war!

Her little groups became busy also finding civilian clothes for the hidden soldiers and taking them what food they could find. Then on 13th June 1940 she heard General De Gaulle's stirring speech to the French nation on the BBC radio and she forthwith made up her mind to join his forces in England. She made her way across France to the foot of the Pyrenees and tried to persuade guides to take her over the mountains to Spain. They asked her how much money she had and when she offered them her entire three hundred francs they laughed. She had to return all the way back but now she went to live with her three old aunts in Paris and got a job in the civil service determined to save up enough money to pay the guides. At night the four of them lacking anything more lethal than white paint used to emerge into the streets and whilst her aunts acted as 'look-outs' she painted anti-German slogans on walls and hoardings and sometimes—if she was lucky—on the sides of sentry boxes.

There were a number of British wounded in hospitals in Paris at the time and Suzanne and a friend started visiting them. Four British Army surgeons were planning an escape at this time and when they knew Suzanne well enough to trust her they confided their plans to her. She brought them in what they wanted and on the occasion of their escape caused a diversion in the hospital so that they got away safely.

The medical staff included two Scottish soldiers, Tommy Edgar and Jimmy Tobin. They were actually soldiers of the 51st Highland Division who had pretended to be medical orderlies when captured. Suzanne now helped them to escape —she brought them civilian clothing. She put a pair of men's trousers on under her skirt and rolled the legs up, as she was passing the sentry of the hospital gate one of the trouser legs started to unroll towards her ankle. For a moment she thought all was lost but with her knees together she managed to totter crabwise around a corner and secure it firmly again. That night the two Scots got out of a lavatory window, climbed down a drainpipe, crossed a garden and emerged onto the street through a private house. Suzanne and a friend were waiting for them. They hid that night in Paris and next morning Suzanne got them false papers and they all travelled into unoccupied France to Marseilles. They went to the British Seaman's Mission which was then being run by the Rev. Donald Caskie, a Scottish clergyman, who was working with the Captain Garrow escape line. He took over the two soldiers who soon afterwards arrived safely back in England.

Suzanne asked if she could also be sent to England as she wanted to join De Gaulle's forces, but she was told that if she wanted to help she would be far more useful stopping in France to guide and assist scores of allied personnel to safety. Few of them could talk French and they were completely dependent on the Resistance for help. She agreed. She was posted as assistant to an Englishman who was carrying out valuable escape-line work on his own and with other groups, and he won her trust and admiration. She concluded several successful missions for him. It was a great blow when he was captured, but he escaped and quickly resumed work.

But then things started to go wrong, and several members of the circuit were arrested, interrogated, tortured and shot. Eventually nearly every member had been eliminated and it was obvious that a traitor was at work.

One day her chief handed her a piece of paper on which was the plan of a German fighter aerodrome near Paris. He told her to take it to Lyon and stop the night in a safe house. Next morning she was to take the plan to a house—he told her the address—and hand it over to the people she would meet there. As she was leaving the safe house next morning she saw two men who looked like policemen approaching. She hurriedly swallowed the piece of paper—an extremely unpleasant and unpalatable tit-bit! They were detectives from the Vichy police and they arrested her and took her to their headquarters. They told her that although they were not working for the Resistance they had discovered the traitor who had betrayed her circuit and that he was being charged for betraying French nationals to the Gestapo. Then they faced her with him—it was her chief! At first she rejected the idea and was convinced it was a trick to get her to talk. She refused to hear anything against him—but he broke down and confessed. When the Gestapo had arrested him some weeks before he had, either through fear or bribery, decided to betray his Resistance colleagues. If the detectives had not stopped Suzanne that morning she too would have been betrayed because the house to which he had directed her with the incriminating plans was run by the Gestapo.

He was sentenced to death by the Vichy court, but was rescued by the Germans for whom he subsequently worked openly. Towards the end of the war he was shot dead by police in Paris. They thought he was one of the German soldiers who stopped behind when the German army left and they wanted to question and possibly detain him. But his guilt complex obliged him to draw a pistol and he fired and wounded one of them; the other shot him dead.

Suzanne continued to work with the escape organization until January 1943 when she was arrested in Lyon by the Gestapo. For two months she was subjected to prolonged and savage interrogation, but they could get nothing out of her so they sent her to a hostage prison at Castres. This was a prison where people whom the Germans would shoot as hostages were kept. She was there from May until September and was lucky enough not to be chosen for any one of the batches of prisoners who were taken and executed as a reprisal against some Resistance activity. She shared a cell there with another SOE woman agent Blanche Charlet.

Then on 16th September 1943 the worms turned! Here is the story as Suzanne told me. 'Some of the prisoners had got hold of pistols through one of the warders who was in the Resistance. They also had duplicate keys of all the cells.

About six o'clock one evening when half the guards were out having their dinner the prisoners held up the other half, knocked them out and locked them in the cells. The prison was in the centre of the town and we had to get out by little groups of three every five minutes, so as not to arouse suspicion. In the meantime some of the guards had been coming back from dinner. They would ring the bell, one of us would open the door and whilst he was closing it, two of the prisoners would jump on the guard with a blanket, knock him out and put him in one of the cells. We were very lucky that none of the guards happened to ring the bell while one of the groups was escaping—it was a chance we had to take.

'I was about the twenty-second or twenty-third to leave with Blanche and a young Alsatian boy who had been put by force in the German Army, escaped, joined the underground and been captured again. In all fifty men and two women escaped, five were recaptured that night and tortured to death.'

The three of them safely reached the country and shortly afterwards the Alsatian boy went off on his own. Suzanne and Blanche walked till 6 a.m. when they reached a village and decided to ask a priest for help, he introduced them to a local farmer but neither of the girls trusted him so they set off again. After two wet days and nights without food or shelter they came to a Benedictine monastery, rang the bell and asked for the Superior. They expected to meet an elderly kindly old man, but Don Emmanuel who came to meet them was young and active—and also kindly. He said they could not hide in the Monastery—no women were allowed there—but that they could live in the guest house in the grounds which was looked after by an aristocratic lady, Mademoiselle Marie Thérèse de la Marguette. The monk said he would also try to contact their British organization.

In Suzanne's own words, 'We stayed at the Monastery for more than two months and the monks were wonderful, I shall never forget their kindness nor that of the old lady. All of them were risking death and torture and maybe even the destruction of the monastery, but they never made us feel that we were like two sticks of dynamite in their hands.'

The monks finally put the two girls in touch with a French network which took them as far as the Pyrenees, but the weather became worse and heavy snow drifts made the journey across the mountains impossible. They returned to the monastery until the French network asked them to become active, so they started work again as couriers and escorts travelling to and from Paris.

In April 1944 London made contact with them and ordered them to return to England. They were taken to Brittany which was in the forbidden coastal zone. At that time the Germans were being very jittery, as they suspected—quite rightly—that the invasion was near.

Suzanne said, 'We were taken into that zone in a small, old-fashioned baker's van which was closed at the back by a piece of tarpaulin which floated in the wind. Had the back been closed the Germans would certainly have suspected it, but it never crossed their mind that anybody would have the nerve to smuggle people in an open van. Hundreds of people went through in that van and, as far as I know, the baker was never caught.

'The van kept on stopping on the roads so that the baker could deliver his bread. Often there were Germans near, but they never looked. We finally drove into a garage and were told to get out and got into a room where we met eighteen other people who were escaping. They had also been smuggled in the baker's van on previous occasions and we were now waiting for a boat from England to pick us up.

'The boat was supposed to come that night and we waited for the message confirming this to come through on the wireless, on the personal messages. It came after the 9 p.m. news. It meant that the boat, motor gun boat 502, would definitely call at a spot on the coast at 2 a.m. These messages were given on the French programme of the BBC and were frequently very funny. I was carrying very important messages at that time and the message that would be sent out to confirm that I had delivered them safely in England was to be 'Patrick fait toujours pipi au lit'. I don't think I will translate, as I blush to say I was the author.

'Blanche and I slept part of the afternoon and then we started getting ready for the trip. Two days before in Paris I had bought a lovely hat with a big white feather. I wore that hat all through our trip and tied it securely to my head with a dark scarf as it would have been dangerous if a Parisian hat was found on the wild moors of Brittany by a German patrol. Everybody in our party teased me for wanting to be elegant on such an expedition, but when we reached England, I was the only one with a smart new hat, although I must admit it was a little battered; my silk stockings were torn to pieces and my coat and dress soaked and the colours faded by sea water. But I had my hat with the white feather! Blanche had bought a bottle of Chanel No. 5 which broke in her bag and in no time at all the fisherman's house instead of smelling of fish, was reeking with Chanel No. 5. We tried everything, opening all doors and windows, making draughts, washing every article in her bag, but it must have been pretty good stuff because when we left that night the house still smelt very strongly of Chanel No. 5.

'So, we started on our way. Along with the eighteen of us going to England were six or eight other men and women who were coming to the beach to help carry the arms, radio sets, baggages, etc. of the agents who were coming to France on that same boat. The fisherman who owned the house where we stayed (the one smelling of Chanel No. 5.) was our guide, and only somebody who had lived there all his life could find his way, mile after mile, without following a path, across the wild moors of Brittany.

'Then we came to a minefield and about every fifteen minutes, he would stop, and the whole column would stop. Every bush looked like a human being and my heart was way up in my throat. In my pockets were two rolls of micro films (photographs of German documents) which I hoped with all my heart I could throw in a bush in case of a fight, as when those things were found on you it meant some very painful scenes of Gestapo "interrogation". In my hand, ready to be swallowed, I had a very important plan which I was told must not be found *on any account* as only one person could possibly have copied it and the Gestapo would have known whom immediately. For certain reasons this objective had to be bombed within eight days or it would be too late. The last time I had been arrested I had to swallow a couple of quite thick pieces of paper so this time I made sure the copy was on very thin air mail paper. After midnight, we got very near the beach and we had to slide down the dunes which was awful for my stockings as we kept on falling and scratching our legs and of course we had to do all that in silence and not even grumble! You could see the person in front of you falling but it was so steep that you had to fall yourself. Finally we got down to the beach, it was tiny, surrounded by cliffs and I certainly take off my hat to the British Navy for finding it in the dark, such a tiny speck of earth and getting there, like perfect gentlemen, exactly on time: 2 a.m. It was about 1 a.m. when we got down there and we sat without talking, smoking or moving. After a while, I was sure two or three times that I could see life boats (the boat stops in the high seas because of the engine noise and sends the life boats).

'My little boats turned out to be rocks. At 2 a.m., the fisherman said, "The boat has arrived, I heard the engine", none of us had heard anything, but I suppose his ears were trained by years and years at sea. Anyway, about thirty minutes later, all of a sudden I saw life boats landing on the beach, they had been rowing so silently that you could not even hear it. And for the first time in nearly four years, after so many green uniforms, I saw good old British uniforms. I wanted to cry, I was so happy. In the meantime, the agents coming ashore had disembarked with all their stuff and we got into the life boats. We were three women, and very gallantly, the British sailors carried us to the boats so that we would not get our feet and legs wet, but they told us to sit in the bottom of the boat which had quite a few inches of sea water! We rowed away in perfect silence to the big boats (two of them had come that night).

'My knowledge of boats is quite limited and I have no idea what they were, they seemed awfully big to me. We climbed along a net which ran on the side of the boat (I still had my hat on!) and got on deck. Quite a few people were waiting for us on deck but nobody talked, some hands pushed us down some stairs, along a corridor and into a cabin. At least, I found out later it was a cabin as it was pitch dark. We stood up like dummies, afraid to move and bang into things. After a while we heard the engine start and then the lights went on in our cabin. I suppose it was perfectly camouflaged from the outside. We were five in that cabin, four men and myself. (Blanche and the other women were on the other boat). An officer from the ship came in and brought us tea and sandwiches; it was wonderful, I felt miles away from the war. However, the tea party did not last long, all of a sudden, we heard the sound of firing outside, but by that time I was so thoroughly sea-sick that I did not care any more what happened. After a few minutes there was no more shooting.

'The next morning I heard there was some trouble with three German boats who fired at us and that one sailor was killed aboard. As soon as it got light two RAF fighters circled the boats. I would have liked to go on deck to see them but I was too sea-sick. We arrived at an English port in the early morning. After making our reports and getting rid, *with pleasure*, of the documents I had been carrying, Blanche and I locked ourselves in the officer's bathroom and took a one-hour bath, the first one we had had in a long time. Then we had a wonderful breakfast, fried eggs, bacon, etc. On top of it we ate some milk chocolate; our stomachs, used to some other kind of diet, protested and we were very sick again. Then we were on our way to London. I volunteered to go back to France and after some leave spent with my English relatives, I joined the F.A.N.Y. and was trained as a radio operator, in guerrilla warfare, sabotage, parachute jumping, etc. and in the middle of all that I found an American husband who was in O.S.S. and was training in the same British military schools as I.'

Suzanne and Blanche Charlet were two of the few SOE agents to be rescued by the Royal Navy. Most of them we have seen arrived by parachute or aircraft and returned by aircraft.

Shortly after the war some of Suzanne's adventures were told in a BBC radio programme I wrote. Afterwards, the naval signalman who was on duty on the boat in which she returned wrote to tell her the full story of the miraculous escape they all had that night. He wrote:

36, The Jordans,
Allesley Park Est.
Coventry.
Sept 11th 1960

Dear Mrs Charise,
After I posted my last letter, I found myself wondering if you would want to be reminded of a period quite long ago. Myself I have never forgotten the lads I served with and the people we took backwards and forwards to Brittany. For myself the story starts 5th July '43, before that I had served in the North Sea and Channel but then I had to report to a boat in Southampton MGB 502, she was brand new with three 1,000 HP Diesels and after being fitted out was a treat to be serving on. We all signed the 'Official Secrets Act' and wondered why!!!

From there on along with four other boats that made up our strange flotilla, one MASB, one C class GB, one D class GB, 502 and 503 having no class being the only two of their type.

Dartmouth became our base and we tied up at all times along an old paddle steamer, her name was the Kinoram. Hush hush was the order of the day and we needed no record tellings on the subject for it was a very interesting game we played, till well after the invasion. We only went to sea to take passengers to Brittany, we made many, many trips, mostly single boats because on such a venture two was a crowd.

That is why on reading about your adventures, the night in question is still fresh in my mind. We would be told to prepare for sea and then strangers would come aboard with suitcases and even bike tyres marked 'made in Belgium'. This night in question two of us made for sea, the D class MGB was with us, we either had a lot of passengers to take or to bring back. The senior boat of the 15th flotilla was my boat 502 so we led. Being the Signalman my station was the bridge, the Captain Lt. Commander Williams would then brief me as to what we might meet.

Sometimes we would have the call sign of a German in the area to use if needed but this night we had no information. We carried first class navigators who with the equipment aboard could I am sure, have found a needle in a hay stack.

On the run in, we cut to one motor and would almost touch bottom before stopping and letting go a rope anchor, we carried two boats for the beach, prams we called them, out they would go and down the scrambling nets would go passengers and boat crew. On board we would be all eyes wanting our chicks to come home as soon as possible. When they did, the passengers would go below and we would have to make for home, this part of the trip was the worst in my opinion, he sometimes traced us entering the area but could do little. On the way out, he had by then a little time to be ready for us. The only time two boats were fired on was the night we brought you across. We had the passengers below and the 'prams' inboard and we made for Dartmouth. We had been under way sometime when the Captain observed boats on the port bow, this was not too good for on the Starboard side were rocks, I think they were called the Grappas, so we could only steer ahead. He had in fact picked a lovely spot to ambush us. All this time I had the telephone set to all guns on my head and the small signal lamp handy.

The Captain told the Coxwain who was on the wheel to hold course and through me warned all guns, the D boat being about two boats length astern, she would follow our move.

By this time we were doing about 20 knots, very steady in fact and the bluff had to begin very soon, eight Jerry boats were there, we knew later they were R boats. They were five on our port bow when we were challenged, I do not know to this day whether it was V ... – or B – ... it came so fast (I was not the only signalman) to feel his blood race that night. Anyway we were ready for such a challenge and the Captain told me to send KA -.-.- which I did, this told the German to wait as would another German ship who had to look up the reply, all of the time we were drawing closer to the gap and away, the longer we could confuse and delay him the better our chances to get home. He finally got fed up of my lamp, he knew who we were anyway and they opened fire. One second I was looking at his lamp, the next to hundreds of tracer moving slowly at first and then terribly fast, it was a dark night and then to have all the tracer, did not help one's vision. The Captain called for emergency speed and ordered open fire. I pressed the open fire button to all guns and told them over the phone to fire, NOTHING happened, not a shot in reply, a dreadful moment I shall never forget, we felt sure on the bridge that all guns had been hit, the D boat didn't fire because we didn't and she fell slightly behind because of our increases in speed, I was not able to tell her of this. We were now thundering along and level with them when they stopped firing as suddenly as they began, seconds later we were on our way home out of it. I was detailed to go visit the guns and check what had happened, I didn't know what I would find so it was a surprise to find only one man had been killed and no one wounded, in fact what had happened was that they could not see to open fire, the tracer after the dark and so close to them had made them blind for some seconds. This in fact saved us because Jerry had real doubts as to who we were when no firing came his way, our monitors picked up his signal to St Malo expressing his concern in case he had fired on his mates. Had he not stopped firing our chances would have been very very slight but we out bluffed him and luck was with us when our Gunners could not see to fire. At dawn we always had two fighters to escort us the last leg home. Bacon and eggs and the next trip to get ready for.

The D boat had one hit astern with no one hurt, our guns did not fire and that saved us, I am sure of that but the

Captain left the lads in no doubt about how he felt when he ordered open fire, how lucky for us they were not able to that night.

I have a large photo of 502 should you like it. As for the lads, the D boat crew should all be OK but my mates on 502 I think only 4 or 5 of us left. Her number was 2002 when she went down on her trip to Norway. The Captain Lt.-Commander Williams was getting a medal when she went down so he will be all right. He was a great chap to have been with, the boat was the best, the crew all good lads and we helped and rubbed shoulders with the bravest there was, people like yourself, we took many to Brittany, it was a job we had but compared to you people we had feather beds all the way. It was a pleasure to have helped you and with pride I remember you all who went on our trips in and out of France.

Yours sincerely
F.G. Colledge

In his first very brief letter, after reading the adventures, Mr Colledge said, 'I was aboard the gun boat that brought you back to Dartmouth, did you realize how nearly we never saw Dartmouth again. The firing you heard was the nearest to "buying it" I had in the two years of these operations. Our flotilla 15 MGBs did nothing else but these trips to Brittany during the no moon periods and we had our share of excitement but this night in April 44 Jerry had made *sure* we would not get back, it is quite a story and I am sure you would like to hear of your and my lucky escape that dark night . . .'

Few people who meet Suzanne and her husband, André, would guess anything about their war-time activities. André served with the American equivalent of SOE—OSS, or the Office of Strategic Services. They met when they were training at an SOE Commando school in Scotland. They are living happily in the south of England—André a talented painter, Suzanne a confirmed book-worm. When they can take time off from the continuous rounds of voluntary charity work in which they are engaged they visit their two grand-children.

Suzanne returns regularly to visit the priest who befriended her and Blanche, her fellow escapee,—Father Don Emmanuel—at his monastery and his neighbour Mademoiselle Marie Thérèse de la Marguette, 'The funny thing was that I went also to visit the prison at Castres but I could not get in—it was much easier getting out!' she told me.

14

MARY FROM SUTTON

All the women mentioned so far were attached to Special Operations Executive and were infiltrated into the field and trained by that organization. There was, however, another highly secret department attached to Army Intelligence which also used women agents in enemy-occupied territories. Mr Airey Neave, a distinguished soldier, incorrigible escaper and now a member of Parliament was attached to that Department, called Room 900, after he had escaped from the high-security German prison, Colditz.

He has written a number of excellent books on some of his experiences including *Saturday at M19* (Saturday was his code name) in which he tells of the stories of some of the women who worked on the escape routes which Room 900 maintained. He has kindly given me permission to recount here the story of one of these women, Mary Lindell, a remarkably adventurous and irrepressible English woman who was born in Sutton, Surrey. When she was old enough she volunteered as a nurse during the First World War, but she found nursing in England rather tame so she transferred to the French Red Cross and served with great distinction in Field hospitals winning many French and British decorations. When that war finished she married and remained living in France with her husband and three children. She was in Paris in 1940 when the German army arrived and became busily engaged in driving sick children across the German demarcation line into unoccupied France.

Later in 1940 Captain J. Windsor-Lewis of the Welsh Guards arrived in Paris by German army lorry—he had thumbed a lift on it. The handsome very English-looking officer had been wounded and captured at Boulogne, but had escaped before his wounds healed and, not speaking a word of French, began a lonely attempt to get back to Britain. He had been lucky enough to meet some sympathetic people who cared for him and when he was fit enough packed him off on his escape attempt. Neither they nor he had any knowledge of official escape groups or routes.

In Paris he made his way to the American Embassy—which was neutral at the time—and vainly tried to convince them that he was an American citizen who had lost his papers. As they turned him away an Englishman named Colonel Cecil Shaw arrived who was married to an American and still living, and helping the underground in Paris. He heard the Captain's story, believed it, and introduced him to Mary Lindell who immediately hid him in her flat and decided to drive him into unoccupied territory. She first had to get a permit from the German authorities to ferry another 'sick child' over the border. She got one which included permission for her to be accompanied by a mechanic. They set out at once and all went well until they were stopped by a young German pilot in flying kit, standing by the side of the road. He asked Mary where she was driving and she told him Orléans, but he got in beside her and told her to drive to Chartres. On the way he told her that he had just been on an abortive bombing mission to Bristol where heavy mist had obscured the target. On the way back his aircraft had been attacked and damaged by a Spitfire and he and his crew had to bail out. Then the pilot looked at the 'mechanic', Windsor-Lewis, sitting in the back and saying nothing and asked Mary who he was. 'My mechanic,' she said. The German said that he did not look very intelligent and Mary agreed saying that he was a little simple-minded.

At Chartres the pilot introduced Mary to the German officer in charge who thanked her for giving the pilot a lift and rewarded her with some petrol coupons. Then the pilot wanted to be driven back to his aerodrome and when they reached there insisted on Mary driving around the perimeter so that she could admire the bombers and fighters. He took her to the Mess for a drink and afterwards waved her good-bye.

Mary's conversation with the pilot had been in English as he knew no French so that her 'simple-minded mechanic' sitting in the back understood everything. Now as they drove away Mary looked at him and saw one sleeve of his shirt was open and displaying the badge of the Welsh Guards tattooed on his forearm! 'For God's sake, sew your damned shirt buttons on in future,' she said.

The rest of the journey went well. With the help of an Irish identity card, which Mary provided, Windsor-Lewis travelled as a neutral to Portugal and from there to London where he made a full report.

Nothing more was known, nor heard, about her until two years later when Mr Airey Neave's department at MI9 were informed from Barcelona in Spain that a woman dressed in the uniform of the French Red Cross with numerous First World War decorations had reported to the British Embassy. She had a British Passport and was named Mary Lindell. She had passed the frontiers as a stranded governess—and now she wanted to be returned to France with a radio operator to start an escape organization.

Mr Neave met her in London soon afterwards. This is how he describes her: 'She was standing in the sunshine, dressed in the royal blue uniform of the French Red Cross with a row of French and British decorations. She was at this time about forty-five, but looked considerably younger. She had dark brown eyes and chestnut hair, and her face was finely proportioned. Her figure was slight and her uniform well cut. She seemed very feminine, but in her expression there was an intensity, a stubbornness which somehow did not fit her smart appearance'. She told him what had happened since the Windsor-Lewis escape. The Gestapo had called at her flat at Christmas and searched it. They had not found her British passport nor a hidden revolver. They called the following day and took her away for questioning—they knew about Colonel Shaw who had introduced her to Windsor-Lewis. After severe questioning they court-martialled her—charged with helping a British officer to escape and insulting the German army. She was found guilty and sentenced to eleven years' hard labour. She asked the President of the court how she had insulted the German army and he said that she had said, 'These swine are going to arrest me'.

She confused the court when she explained that in English the word 'swine' did not mean pig, but a wild boar; a splendid animal of courage and ferocity. It was a praiseworthy description. Then her counsel handed up her citation in 1916 for the Croix de Guerre and the officer who read it stood up and saluted her. So it was read to the court and they all stood up and saluted her. They also reduced her sentence to nine months' solitary confinement. This so amused her that she said, 'Just sufficient time for me to have a baby with Adolf'.

'What did she say?' the President asked and her counsel hurriedly interpreted it as, 'in the circumstances she considers the sentence fair'.

She spent the nine months in the Fresnes prison and then with the help of an American vice-consul made her escape to Barcelona. The Germans missed her in France and put her on their wanted list. In spite of this she was adamant that she should return there and MI9 eventually agreed that after a brief training she should go to the town of Rufflec in an area where it was known there were usually a number of allied airmen waiting to make their escape to Britain.

On 20th October 1942 she was taken to France by Lysander and immediately began organizing an escape route, but then she received a serious set-back. One night riding a tandem bicycle a motor car ran into the back and she was knocked unconscious and so badly injured that villagers thought she was dead and began to dig her grave. Luckily, a French chemist arrived, pronounced her alive and she was taken to hospital secretly and hidden there. The Germans heard about the accident and searched the hospital, but did not find her in the cellar where her bed was hidden behind a load of wood.

Whilst she was still ill she became involved in the escape of two members of the Royal Marines who survived the famous

'Cockleshell Heroes' Commando raid of December 1942. Then twelve members of the Royal Marine Boom Patrol Detachment, including the Commanding Officer, Lieut.-Colonel (Blondie) Hazler, set off from a submarine in fifteen-foot-long two-man canoes to paddle ninety miles up the River Gironde in southern France to attack merchant shipping in Bordeaux harbour. Only two canoes reached the target area, the occupants of the other nine canoes were either captured and shot out-of-hand by the Germans or drowned, one canoe was found to be holed when launched from the submarine so its crew did not set out. Canoe 'Catfish' manned by Lieut-Colonel H.G. Hazler and Marine Bill Sparks attached limpet-mines to six ships; canoe 'Crayfish', manned by Corporal Laver and Marine Mills attached their bombs to two ships.

The two crews met immediately afterwards and, acting on their instructions, scuttled their canoes and set off on foot to make their separate ways back to England. Laver and Mills were never heard of again, Hazler and Sparks walked a hundred miles to the town of Rufflec. All the limpet-mines went off causing tremendous damage and infuriating Hitler.

Official policy had decreed that none of the Commandoes should be given the names and addresses of anybody connected with the Resistance or escape routes. This was to ensure that should any of them be captured the Germans could not obtain such information from them. Indeed, the Resistance knew nothing at all about the plans to attack the Bordeaux shipping and were about to do it when the Marines made that unnecessary. But Hazler and Sparks had been told to make their way, if possible, to Rufflec where they would find friends. They were not told that Mary Lindell operated from there and they came to her notice through a piece of rare good luck—just by going into a café and discreetly telling the waiter that they were British soldiers trying to escape. They were passed on to Mary's organization and eventually met her. Alhough still very ill from her accident she had left hospital. On their first meeting she had insisted upon Lieut.-Colonel Hazler's prominent blond moustache being cut off with scissors. She hid them in Lyon whilst she sought a way to smuggle them out of the country and, in spite of her injuries, made her way across the frontier to Switzerland bringing to the British Legation there the first news of their escape. The British officials there tried to keep her until she was fully fit but she ignored them and returned to Lyon where she arranged for a guide to take the two marines over the Pyrenees to Spain, from where they soon arrived in England.

Subsequently Mary was busily engaged on her escape line until she was captured by the German security services in November 1943. She was interrogated in Biarritz and then put on the train, under escort, for Paris. On the way she dived from the train, the German guard fired, one bullet hitting her in the back of the head, another went through her cheek. The Germans operated on her, saved her life, and put her to prison in Dijon where for eight months she received savage treatment. Then they sent her to the dreadful women's concentration camp at Ravensbruck in Germany in September 1944, and she was liberated from there on 3rd April 1945. Whilst at Ravensbruck she worked ceaselessly and unselfishly for the other women prisoners—saving several from the gas-chamber, including one of the SOE girls.

Now over seventy she is living in Paris and still engaged in helping people in need.

We have seen how these girls played an active part in the total warfare that was waged in France between 1940 and 1944. Their task was to assist the French resistance and in doing so none of them shrank from their own utter commitment—even unto torture and death. What did they accomplish?

The overall Chief of the Secret Armies of Britain was General Sir Colin Gubbins, KGMC, DSO, MC. Three years after the war finished, in January 1948, when enough time had passed to collate and evaluate the work of SOE in France he delivered a lecture on the work of the Resistance movements at the Royal United Service Institute in London. He, more than anybody else, knew the value of work done and the enormous part it played in eventual victory. He was kind enough to give me permission to reproduce the following excerpts from his lecture. Sir Colin said that sabotage targets were not picked at random, but after full examination and discussion with the various departments concerned and that in France constant destruction was wrought against vital points in the German war economy and he quoted these few scattered examples:

> The destruction of the Ratier Air Screw factory at Toulouse; the destruction of the power supply arrangements for Le Greusot—the biggest armament works in France; the demolition of the Gigny barrage on the Sâone, holding up the German E-boat traffic to the Mediterranean for five critical weeks. This operation was repeated the following year: the demolition of Radio-Paris, used for jamming and propaganda, innumerable power stations and transformers and continuous rail attacks, particularly against supply trains carrying oil to submarine bases.
>
> He went on: 'As far as clandestine operations in France were concerned, the British Government retained direct responsibility for operations. This position was maintained until the invasion of Normandy, when all clandestine forces in France, whether led by British or built up by General De Gaulle under the guidance and control of the British, were placed by General Eisenhower under the command of General Koenig, a very right and proper arrangement. That was the proper culmination of French resistance—the resurgence of France as a great Power and her open participation again in the war—factors of immense importance for the future.
>
> 'Thus from the moment of the fall of France, and the commencement of total warfare against Germany, British officers and others, after due training, were parachuted into occupied territories to start the organization of resistance. As regards France, no one knew, no one could tell, how many Frenchmen were for De Gaulle or how many for Vichy and subservience; but we knew that thousands would help the British and waited only for the chance to fight the aggressor and harass him wherever possible, and so we went

ahead. Information gradually obtained showed that De Gaulle had a strong following and soon he was given facilities for beginning the creation of a secret army—a process that was to continue for three and a half years with varying turns of fortune but steadily improving position.

'For overriding reasons of operational security, the control of signals traffic and of the training and despatching of personnel remained with SOE and the teams in the field were organized as far as possible on the British model into close water-tight compartments each with its specific area and specific targets, whether for sabotage or for the day of invasion. And so SOE had two sections for France—one for the British "circuits" as they were known, and the other directing and checking the creation of a secret army that would follow De Gaulle, and in which quite a number of British officers took part.

'There were, therefore, particular difficulties in dealing with France—the absence of any recognized authority outside France, the initial division into two zones—Occupied and Unoccupied, and so on. On the other hand, there were many physical and concrete advantages which France possessed. First there was the wide extent of the country, which is relatively not highly populated, so that the finding of suitable dropping grounds was not very difficult and even pick-up operations by aircraft at night were fairly simple once the technique had been evolved. Secondly, the run for the aircraft was comparatively short, so that maximum container loads were almost always possible. Thirdly, France could be approached both from north and south, i.e. from bases in England and Algiers, so that even on the shortest summer nights there was practically no point that could not be reached, though the short summer nights in the Western Theatre were always a problem. A further factor helping French operations was that, compared say with Holland, Belgium, Czechoslovakia or Poland, it was relatively easy to get selected important people back to this country for consultation; there was the aircraft pick-up method; there were the land frontiers and the long coast lines facing England and North Africa.

'The invasion of North Africa brought about, of course, another simplification—France was no longer divided into two zones—Occupied and Unoccupied. Two peoples—one suffering under Occupation and the other suffering only under Vichy, became totally Occupied and the French resistance by that much hardened and crystallized.

'The history of the building up of the secret armies in France, as in other western European countries though to a lesser degree, was studded with sudden arrests of key men, with discovery of our W/T sets and setbacks of all kinds. But the work was gradually accomplished in spite of a tendency towards centralization and the building up of a military hierarchy, the dangers of which in warfare of this kind are obvious; if the head of a zone is caught with his executive records, tremendous damage will ensue; this happened more than once. Numbers to be built up were decided more by the availability of aircraft to deliver equipment and arms than the numbers willing to serve; the governing factor was not the available supplies but the rate of and volume in which they could be delivered.

'From February 1944 until the end of the first phase of the Allied invasion, special efforts were made for France, using not only aircraft allotted for SOE work but additional aircraft from Bomber and Transport Command. From February to May alone, arms for sixty-thousand men were safely delivered throughout the length and breadth of France, but mostly to the Maquis of the central and south-east, and then after May to the northern sectors which had such an immediate bearing on the Normandy invasion. The weather played an important role in the selection of delivery points. In March alone, there were two hundred successful sorties to the Maquis—a formidable total.

'As 6th June approached, so the pressure for deliveries grew, and so also grew the need for precision both as regards time and place in what was being done. The invasion was planned for Normandy, and all Resistance plans had to be aimed at giving the maximum assistance to the initial landing and then to the build-up. Therefore plans had to be sent in advance to France in the shape of micro-films. Whether they concerned railway sabotage, destruction of telephones and W/T communications, or whatever they might be, it was imperative that their possible capture by the Germans should not in any way prejudice the security of operations—in fact, that the most minute examination of those plans should not give any indication as to whether the action was to be mounted across the narrow straits, or on Dieppe and so to Calais, or west of the Seine, i.e. Normandy or Bordeaux, or the Flemish coasts and Antwerp. So all operational directives were worked out with SHAEF to cover these points and to maintain secure the aspect of 'locality of the invasion'.

'But what of time? If Resistance were to help, it must be synchronized, and if the Germans could not deduce place, the deduction of 'time' would be of some advantage to them. To cover this point, a relatively simple 'stand by' code was evolved which if picked up by the Germans would tell them nothing, but conveyed to the "Field" that they should be on the look out for the "Action" messages. Remember that by 1st June all sorts of things had happened giving clear indications to the Germans that invasion was imminent. And so the "Action" messages went off on 5th June, calling French Resistance to commence action that same evening.

'For SOE this was the most critical point of the War—had this job of primary importance been done? To date this could only rest on faith or conjecture. The weapons, the organization, the plan were all there ready—our one thought was how it would go on the day. The answer is a matter of history. The 'Plan Vert'—the green plan, for railway demolition started at once. Within the first week of the invasion, 960 railway demolitions out of a planned 1,055 had been well and truly carried out; similarly with communication and road demolitions; and the fighting behind the lines began. By August, 668 locomotives had been destroyed and 2,900 attacks on railways carried out in France alone. Our embarrassment was then to prevent a premature *levée en masse*, a rising of the French people. In this we were not wholly successful, particularly in the case of certain groups in the south of France who fought too early and suffered heavy casualties before the launching of the operation under Field-Marshal Lord Wilson from North Africa. This swept like a wind through southern France and up the valley of the Rhône to the German frontier and hemmed in once and for all the German forces struggling to escape from Bordeaux and Toulouse and the south-west of France, before the net should finally trap them all, as it eventually did. The French forces of the Interior came out into the open; thousands flocked to join and there was no way of stopping them.

'Thus began the bloody battles in the Correze, in Vercors and in Savoie which at first involved heavy losses to the French though producing a valuable diversion from Normandy, but which three months later saw the FFI still unconquered. In June 1944 the Germans were employing 5,000 men against Correze, 11,000 with artillery against Vercors, and on 20th July the 11th Panzer Division wanted in Normandy was still in Dordogne.

'The organized risings, worked out on SHAEF instructions, were so immediately effective that on 25th June the first daylight drop of arms in direct support of overt resistance was carried out—76 Fortresses, a diversion from the main battle front which was judged by General Eisenhower to be warranted. This was followed on 14th July by a daylight sortie of 400 Fortresses, and feeling in France rose to fever height. After that there was no stopping them.

'What did all this achieve? Remember that its object was directly to assist the landings in Normandy and the eventual break-out, i.e. (1) to delay the arrival of reinforcements and (2) to divert troops that might otherwise be used as reinforcements.

'I will quote from an extract from a SHAEF paper of 1944:

'The action of the resistance groups south of the River

Loire resulted in an average delay of 48 hours in the movement of reinforcements to Normandy and often much longer. The enemy was facing a battlefield behind his lines'.

'I would like to quote further an extract from a personal letter from General Eisenhower in May 1945:

'While no final assessment of the operational value of resistance action has yet been completed, I consider that the disruption of enemy rail communications, the harassing of German road moves and the continual and increasing strain placed on German war economy and internal security services throughout Occupied Europe by the organized forces of Resistance, played a very considerable part in our complete and final victory.

The final military conclusions on the subject were:

'Militarily, organized Resistance helped the main operations of the Allied Expeditionary Force as follows:

(a) By sapping the enemy's confidence in his own security and flexibility of internal movement.

(b) By diverting enemy troops to internal security duties and keeping troops thus employed dispersed.

(c) By causing delay to the movement of enemy troops:

(1) concentrating against the Normandy beach-head.

(2) regrouping after the Allied break-out from the beach-head.

(d) By disrupting enemy tele-communications in France and Belgium.

(e) By enabling Allied formations to advance with greater speed through being able to dispense with many normal military precautions, e.g. flank protection and mopping up.

(f) By furnishing military intelligence.

(g) By providing organized groups of men in liberated areas able to undertake static guard duties at short notice and without further training.

The widespread and continuous sabotage (3,000 confirmed

rail cuts between 6th and 27th June) in this field, caused an effect outside the capabilities of Allied air effort unless it had been concentrated on railways to the exclusion of other priority tasks ... It succeeded in imposing more or less serious delays on all the divisions moved to Normandy from the Mediterannean and forced extensive and intricate detours. The stimulation of resistance in Brittany also delayed moves from that area ... An outstanding example was the delay to the 2nd S.S. Panzer Division which took two weeks to reach the bridgehead at a crucial time. The main line Toulouse-Tours was virtually closed to German traffic from D-day onward. Both main lines up to the Rhône Valley were closed a good part of the time, the route on the right bank at one time for twenty consecutive days by the destruction of the Doux bridge at Tournon. Resistance action in Belgium which began on 8th June 1944, completed the wide encirclement of the beach-head. Sabotage to the principal rail routes imposed delay not only on troops moving from that country but on reinforcements and stores passing through it from Germany. Constant interruptions were caused on all other lines in France, particularly those capable of carrying heavy tanks, with the consequence that many Tiger tanks from the South finally had to be moved by road and arrived in the battle area too late and not in fighting condition. Troops likewise arrived in a state of extreme disorganization and exhaustion'.

The story of the southern invasion of France was the same—a constant battlefield behind the lines. In all, between Normandy and the Côte d'Azur, between ten and twelve German divisions hopelessly cut off and blocked, surrendered, to French Resistance. The cost to the French was considerable: 24,000 men killed, but France had regained her soul. Some 300,000 of her citizens in organized formations had sprung to the call of arms.

BIBLIOGRAPHY

Nancy Wake Russell Braddon (Cassell 1956)
Horned Pigeon George Millar (Heinemann 1946)
Carve Her Name with Pride R.J. Minney (Newnes 1956)
Death be not Proud Elizabeth Nicholas (Cresset Press 1958)
Madeleine Jean Overton Fuller (Gollancz 1952)
Odette Jerrard Tickell (Chapman & Hall 1949)
Moondrop to Gascony Ann Marie Walters (Macmillan 1946)
FANY Invicta Dame Irene Ward (Hutchinson 1955)
SOE in France M.R.D. Foot (HMSO 1966)
They Came from the Sky E.H. Cookridge (Heinemann)
Inside SOE E.H. Cookridge (Arthur Barker 1966)
Saturday at MI9 Airey Neave MP (Hodder & Stoughton)
Now It CAN be Told James Gleeson & Tom Waldron (Paul Elek 1950)

A PLACE TO LIVE AND A PLACE TO DIE
By LASZLO DEUTSCH and HARRY BRODIE

Shoshana Ishboneh had lost her first husband and two children in the gas ovens of Europe in 1944. After the war she remarried, moved to Israel and started to build a new life. The two sons born of this second marriage, Uri and Gadi, were growing into fine young men with promising futures—and then came another war. . . .

With both her sons fighting at the front, Shoshana faced tragedy for the second time.

0 552 10283 0—**75p**

CROSS OF IRON
By WILLI HEINRICH

Sergeant Steiner was in command of ten men—survivors of a German rearguard trapped fifty miles behind the Russian lines. Their path to freedom led straight through the whole Russian army, together with all the murderous hazards of war—hunger, exhaustion, treachery, death. In the end, Steiner and his men were no longer fighting for Führer or Fatherland, but for their naked, desperate lives. . . .

0 552 10343 8—**75p**